Instant Pot Duo Crisp Air Fryer Cookbook For Beginners:

Easy and Tasty Instant Pot Duo Crisp +Air Fryer Recipes.

D1519535

by
Sophia Bexley

Contents

Introduction

We all try to cook on a budget. But what about saving time when cooking? Time is money, and there's none to waste. So, will you believe me if I tell you, you can save both time and money whilst cooking all your favorite dishes? Get the Instant Pot Duo Crisp 11 in 1.

It is the latest invention from the makers of the genius Duo series. It has a variety of functions established to make your life easy. As the name suggests, this incredible product boasts 11 various purposes. That's like replacing 11 gadgets with only 1! How amazing is that? This guide will help you recognize the basics of everything you need to know about the Instant Pot Duo Crisp 11 in 1.

What does it do?

The Instant Pot Duo Crisp 11 in 1 comes with a pressure cooker lid and an air fryer lid. You can use each top for a variety of things. For example, the function of the pressure cooker lid is to pressurize your food to cook. In addition, you can also use it to slow cook, sauté ingredients, steam, sous vide, or heat your meals.

On the other hand, you can use the air fryer lid to promptly air fry, roast, broil, bake and desiccate your ingredients. Moreover, you can cook juicy chicken wings, crispy fries and sizzling onion rings, mouth-watering spring rolls, and a lot more 70% faster than other methods. Yet, there's more to come. You can make your cooking experience a lot easier with its numerous one-touch controls and preset cooking functions.

What can you use it for?

To sum up its culinary functions, you can use it for:

- **Pressure Cooking:** This program allows you to pressurize food with steam. It ensures that your dish is cooked evenly and deeply. This way, you'll get predictable and delicious results every time. You can use it for cooking fish and seafood, soft vegetables, rice, eggs, meat, poultry, roots and other hard vegetables, oats, beans, grains, bone broth, and chili. In addition, you can choose between high and low temperatures. The maximum cooking time is 4 hours.

- **Air frying:** You can use this feature to air fry fresh or frozen fries, chicken wings, and shrimp. The average time required is about 18 minutes. Although, there's a default temperature. You can change it anywhere between what the range allows (180°F–400°F or 82°C–204°C).

- **Roasting**: it takes approximately 40 minutes for Instant Pot Duo Crisp 11 in 1 to roast your food. The default temperature is 380°F or 193°C. Although, you can adjust it at any time.

- **Baking**: You can use its Bake Smart Program to create decadent brownies, light, fluffy cakes, pastries, buns, puffy cakes, and so much more!

- **Broiling**: Broiling requires direct top-down heating, and broiled foods benefit when placed close to the element. You can use it to melt cheese on French onion soup or nachos, etc.

- **Dehydrating**: The Dehydrate Smart Program applies low heat over a long period to safely dry out food items. It is typically used to make fruit leather or jerky and dried vegetables. However, remember not to crowd the multi-level air fryer basket or the broil/dehydrating tray, because the air should be able to circulate freely around food items.

- **Sauté**: The Sauté Smart Program is quite like using a frying pan, skillet, or flat-top grill. You can use Sauté to simmer, reduce and thicken liquids, stir-fry foods, or caramelize vegetables and sear meat before or after cooking. When you sauté meat and vegetables before pressure cooking, it boosts flavors. Moreover, deglazing can help give your recipes extra depth. Use it for simmering, reducing, thickening, and caramelizing meals. In addition, you can also pan sear, stir-fry, sauté, and brown foods with it.

- **Slow cook**: this program is comparable to the cooking process of typical slow cookers. It is compatible with any everyday recipe that requires slow cooking.

- **Sous vide**: this kind of cooking brings vacuum-sealed food to an exact temperature. It maintains that temperature for an extended period of time to achieve high quality and consistently delicious results.

What are its products and parts?

The Instant Pot Duo Crisp 11 in 1 consists of several parts and products. You should always verify on opening if all the accessories are available or not. What it contains is:

- **Pressure Cooking Lid**: This lid has a top and interior. The top contains features like Float Valve, Quick Release Button, Lid Handle, Lid Position, Steam Release Valve, and Marker Lid Fins. The interior consists of a Lid Locking Pin, Float Valve, Silicone Cap, Anti-Block Shield, Steam Release Pipe (beneath anti-block shield), Sealing Ring, and Rack Sealing Ring.

- **Air Fryer Lid**: The air fryer has a front, interior, and back. Each with its own features. The front is equipped with lid handles, lid position markers, and lid fins. Next, we have the interior. The interior is an element cover. Below the element cover, there is an element heater. It also contains a male power and sensor connector. Finally, we have the back, which is equipped with an air vent and air intake.

- **Inner Pot**: It also has an inner pot. The pot is made from stainless steel and has a tri-ply bottom. Moreover, it has full line indicators to measure water or broth amounts.

- **Cooker Base**: The cooker base contains a Female Power, Sensor Connector, Outer Pot, Heating Element (interior), Condensation Rim, Control Panel, power cord, and handles to hold it. Remember to never put any food or liquid directly in the cooker base; use the inner pot for that.

- **Other accessories**: other equipment it contains is Broil/Dehydrating Tray, Multi-Level Air Fryer Basket, Air Fryer Basket Base, and Protective Pad and Storage Cover.

What are its controls?

The Instant Pot Duo Crisp 11 in 1 is a reasonably priced product with many functions and controls. You can access these features just by pressing a button on the control panel. These features include:

- **Temperature and pressure display**: the pressure cooker lid indicates the temperature in Lo or Hi values. At the same time, the air fryer shows the precise temperature in degrees Celsius or Fahrenheit.

- **Smart Programs**: You can access the smart programs of both pressure cooker lid and air fryer through this.

- **Smart Program Settings**: this includes features like increasing or decreasing temperature, increasing, or decreasing time, Delay Start, Keep Warm, Cancel and Start.

- **LED Indicators:** These indicators illuminate to indicate which active Smart Program or settings are selected.

How to clean it?

The best thing about this product is how easy it is to clean. All you need to do is get some water and a dishwasher to get to cleaning. However, since it's an electrical product, there are some precautions you must follow.

Disassemble your air fryer before cleaning. You have to rinse it after every use. But don't use any harsh chemicals or detergents for this purpose. Although it is optional, try spraying non-stick cooking oil before using your air fryer. Finally, remember to empty and rinse the condensation collector after each use. These instructions are applicable on:

- Multifunctional Rack

- Condensation Collector

- Protective Pad and Storage Cover

- Multi-Level Air Fryer Basket

- Air Fryer Basket Base

- Broil/Dehydrating Tray

- Condensation Collector

To clean your inner pot, simply use water and detergent. Of course, you have to wash it after every use too. But if the stains are persistent. For example, there is hard water staining. Then you'll have to use vinegar and a scrubber to clean it. However, if there is burnt food, simply let it soak in water for a few hours before washing. Make sure the pot is completely dry before putting it in the cooking base.

Finally, to clean the pressure cooker lid and its parts, take some hot water, mild soap and wash thoroughly after every use. You ought to let it fully dry before placing it back in the product. Do not forget to remove all parts from the lid before dishwashing. Once you are done, rotate the lid 360° to get rid of all the water. Finally, put the sealing ring in a well-ventilated area to decrease the residual odor of flavorful meals.

Candied Lemon Peel

Prep time: 15 minutes | Cook time: 40 minutes | Serves: 15 | Program: Pressure | Per Serving: Calories 36

Ingredients:

- Lemons – 1 lb.
- Water – 5 C. divided
- White sugar – 2¼ C. divided

Directions:

1) Slice the lemon in half lengthwise and extract the juice. Discard the juice.
2) Slice each half in quarters, and with a melon-baller, remove the pulp. Cut the lemon quarters into thin strips.
3) In the pot of Instant Pot Duo Crisp, place the lemon peel strips and 4 C. of water.
4) Cover the pot with "Pressure Lid" and seal it.
5) Press "Pressure" and set the time for 3 minutes.
6) Press "Start" to begin cooking.
7) When cooking time is completed, do a "Natural" release.
8) Open the lid and strain the lemon peel strips. Rinse the strips completely.

9) Remove water from the pot, and with paper towels, pat dry it.
10) In the pot of Instant Pot Duo Crisp, place the lemon peel strips, 1 C. of sugar and 1 C. of water and press "Sauté".
11) Press "Start" to begin cooking and cook for about 5 minutes.
12) Press "Cancel" to stop cooking and stir the mixture well.
13) Cover the pot with "Pressure Lid" and seal it.
14) Press "Pressure" and set the time for 10 minutes.
15) Press "Start" to begin cooking.
16) When cooking time is completed, do a "Natural" release.
17) Open the lid and strain the peel strips.
18) Spread the peel strips onto a cutting board for about 15-20 minutes.
19) Coat the lemon strips with remaining sugar, shaking off the excess.
20) Arrange the lemon strips onto a sheet pan and refrigerate, uncovered for at least 4 hours or overnight before serving.

Caramelized Almonds

Prep time: 10 minutes | Cook time: 20 minutes | Serves: 6 | Program: Air Fry | Per Serving: Calories 152

Ingredients:

- Almonds – 1½ C.

- Egg white – 2 tbsp.
- Powdered sugar – 2 tbsp.
- Ground cinnamon – ½ tbsp.
- Pinch of cayenne pepper

Directions:

1) In a bowl, add all the ingredients and toss to coat well.
2) Arrange the greased Air Fryer Basket in the pot of Instant Pot Duo Crisp.
3) Cover the pot with "Air Fryer Lid" and seal it.
4) Press "Air Fry" and set the temperature to 320 °F for 20 minutes.
5) Press "Start" to begin preheating.
6) When the unit shows "Hot" instead of "On", open the lid and place the almonds into the basket.
7) Again, seal the lid and press "Start" to begin cooking.
8) While cooking, stir the almonds once halfway through.
9) When cooking time is completed, open the lid, and transfer the almonds into a bowl.
10) Set aside to cool before serving.

Spicy Chickpeas

Prep time: 5 minutes | Cook time: 10 minutes | Serves: 4 | Program: Air Fry | Per Serving: Calories 146

Ingredients:

- Chickpeas – 1 (15-oz.) can, rinsed and drained
- Olive oil – 1 tbsp.
- Ground cumin – ½ tsp.
- Cayenne pepper – ½ tsp.
- Smoked paprika – ½ tsp.
- Salt, as required

Directions:

1) In a bowl, add all the ingredients and toss to coat well.
2) Arrange the Air Fryer Basket in the pot of Instant Pot Duo Crisp.
3) Cover the pot with "Air Fryer Lid" and seal it.
4) Press "Air Fry" and set the temperature to 390 °F for 10 minutes.
5) Press "Start" to begin preheating.
6) When the unit shows "Hot" instead of "On", open the lid and place the chickpeas in basket.
7) Again, seal the lid and press "Start" to begin cooking.
8) When cooking time is completed, open the lid, and transfer the chickpeas into a bowl.
9) Serve warm.

Apple Chips

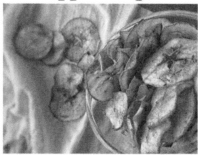

Prep time: 10 minutes | Cook time: 8 hours | Serves: 4 | Program: Dehydrate | Per Serving: Calories 63

Ingredients:

- Red apples – 2, peeled, cored, and thinly sliced
- Sugar – 1 tbsp.
- Ground cinnamon – 1 tsp.

Directions:

1) Place the apple slices into the Dehydrating Tray in a single layer.
2) Arrange the tray in the pot of Instant Pot Duo Crisp.
3) Close the Instant Pot Duo Crisp with "Air Fryer Lid" and Select "Dehydrate".
4) Set the temperature to 150 °F for 8 hours.
5) Press "Start" to begin cooking.
6) When cooking time is completed, open the lid, and transfer the apple slices into a bowl.
7) Add the cinnamon, sugar and toss to coat well.
8) Set aside to cool before serving.

Spinach Chips

Prep time: 10 minutes | Cook time: 10 minutes | Serves: 3 | Program: Air Fry | Per Serving: Calories 49

Ingredients:

- Fresh baby spinach leaves – 4 C.
- Olive oil – 1 tbsp.

- Cayenne pepper – 1/8 tsp.
- Salt and ground black pepper, as required

Directions:

1) In a bowl, add all the ingredients and toss to coat well.
2) Arrange the greased Air Fryer Basket in the bottom of Instant Pot Duo Crisp.
3) Cover the pot with "Air Fryer Lid" and seal it.
4) Press "Air Fry" and set the temperature to 300 °F for 10 minutes.
5) Press "Start" to begin preheating.
6) When the unit shows "Hot" instead of "On", open the lid and place the spinach leaves into the basket.
7) Again, seal the lid and press "Start" to begin cooking.
8) When cooking time is completed, open the lid, and transfer the spinach chips onto a baking sheet for about 5-10 minutes.
9) Serve warm.

Zucchini Fries

Prep time: 15 minutes | Cook time: 10 minutes | Serves: 4 | Program: Air Fry | Per Serving: Calories 158

Ingredients:

- Zucchini – 1 lb. sliced into 2½-inch sticks
- Salt, as required

20

- Olive oil – 2 tbsp.
- Breadcrumbs – ¾ C.

Directions:

1) In a colander, add the zucchini and sprinkle with salt.
2) Set aside for about 10 minutes.
3) Gently pat dry the zucchini sticks with the paper towels and coat with oil.
4) In a shallow dish, place the breadcrumbs.
5) Coat the zucchini sticks with the breadcrumbs evenly.
6) Arrange the greased Air Fryer Basket in the bottom of Instant Pot Duo Crisp.
7) Cover the pot with "Air Fryer Lid" and seal it.
8) Press "Air Fry" and set the temperature to 425 °F for 10 minutes.
9) Press "Start" to begin preheating.
10) When the unit shows "Hot" instead of "On", open the lid and place the zucchini sticks into the basket.
11) Again, seal the lid and press "Start" to begin cooking.
12) When cooking time is completed, open the lid, and serve warm.

Mozzarella Sticks

Prep time: 15 minutes | Cook time: 12 minutes | Serves: 3 | Program: Air Fry | Per Serving: Calories 162

Ingredients:

- All-purpose flour – 3 tbsp.
- Eggs – 2
- Milk – 3 tbsp.
- Breadcrumbs – ½ C.
- Mozzarella cheese block – ½ lb. cut into 3x½-inch sticks

Directions:

1) In a shallow dish, place the flour.
2) In a second shallow dish, add the eggs and milk and beat well.
3) In a third shallow dish, place the breadcrumbs.
4) Coat the Mozzarella sticks with flour, then dip in egg mixture and finally, coat with the breadcrumbs.
5) Arrange the Mozzarella sticks onto a cookie sheet and freeze for about 1-2 hours.
6) Arrange the greased Air Fryer Basket in the pot of Instant Pot Duo Crisp.
7) Cover the pot with "Air Fryer Lid" and seal it.
8) Press "Air Fry" and set the temperature to 400 °F for 12 minutes.
9) Press "Start" to begin preheating.
10) When the unit shows "Hot" instead of "On", open the lid and place the mozzarella sticks into the basket.
11) Again, seal the lid and press "Start" to begin cooking.
12) When cooking time is completed, open the lid, and transfer the mozzarella sticks onto a platter.
13) Serve warm.

Potato Croquettes

Prep time: 15 minutes | Cook time: 8 minutes | Serves: 4 | Program: Air Fry | Per Serving: Calories 283

Ingredients:

- Medium russet potatoes – 2, peeled and cubed
- All-purpose flour – 2 tbsp.
- Parmesan cheese – ½ C. grated
- Egg yolk – 1
- Fresh chives – 2 tbsp. minced
- Pinch of ground nutmeg
- Salt and ground black pepper, as required
- Eggs – 2
- Breadcrumbs – ½ C.
- Vegetable oil – 2 tbsp.

Directions:

1) In a pan of boiling water, add the potatoes and cook for about 15 minutes.
2) Drain the potatoes well and transfer into a large bowl.
3) With a potato masher, mash the potatoes and set aside to cool completely.
4) In the bowl of mashed potatoes, add the flour, Parmesan cheese, egg yolk, chives, nutmeg, salt, and black pepper and mix until well combined.

23

5) Make small cylinder-shaped croquettes from the mixture.
6) In a shallow dish, crack the eggs and beat well.
7) In another dish, mix together the breadcrumbs, and oil.
8) Dip the croquettes in egg mixture and then coat with the breadcrumbs mixture.
9) Arrange the greased Air Fryer Basket in the pot of Instant Pot Duo Crisp.
10) Cover the pot with "Air Fryer Lid" and seal it.
11) Press "Air Fry" and set the temperature to 390 °F for 8 minutes.
12) Press "Start" to begin preheating.
13) When the unit shows "Hot" instead of "On", open the lid and place the croquettes into the basket.
14) Again, seal the lid and press "Start" to begin cooking.
15) When cooking time is completed, open the lid transfer the croquettes onto a platter.
16) Serve warm.

Glazed Chicken Wings

Prep time: 15 minutes | Cook time: 15 minutes | Serves: 4 | Program: Pressure/ Air Fry | Per Serving: Calories 346

Ingredients:

- Chicken wings – 1½ lb.
- Tomato puree – ¼ C.

- Honey – 1 tbsp.
- Fresh lemon juice – 1 tbsp.
- Salt and ground black pepper, as required

Directions:

1) In the pot of Instant Pot Duo Crisp, pour 1 C. of water.
2) Arrange the Multi-Functional Rack in Instant Pot Duo Crisp.
3) Place chicken wings on top of rack, standing vertically.
4) Cover the pot with "Pressure Lid" and seal it.
5) Press "Pressure" and set the time for 10 minutes.
6) Press "Start" to begin cooking.
7) When cooking time is completed, do a "Quick" release.
8) Meanwhile, in a bowl, add remaining ingredients and beat until well combined.
9) Open the lid and coat the wings with sauce generously.
10) Discard the water from the pot of Instant Pot Duo Crisp.
11) Again, arrange the rack in the pot.
12) Place chicken wings on top of rack.
13) Now, cover the pot with "Air Fryer Lid" and seal it.
14) Press "Air Fry" and set the temperature to 400 °F for 5 minutes.
15) Press "Start" to begin cooking.
17) When cooking time is completed, open the lid, and serve hot.

Teriyaki Chicken Wings

Prep time: 15 minutes | Cook time: 19 minutes | Serves: 8 | Program: Pressure/ Broil | Per Serving: Calories 450

Ingredients:

- Chicken wings – 3 lb. drumettes and wings separated
- Olive oil – 6 tbsp. divided
- Teriyaki sauce – 1 C.
- Brown sugar – 1 tbsp.
- Red pepper flakes – ½ tsp. crushed

Directions:

1) In a large bowl, add the chicken wings, 4 tbsp. of oil, teriyaki sauce and brown sugar and mix well.
2) Refrigerate for at least 2 hours.
3) Remove chicken wings from bowl, reserving marinade.
4) In the pot of Instant Pot Duo Crisp, place the remaining oil and press "Sauté".
5) Press "Start" to begin cooking and heat for about 2-3 minutes.
6) Now add the chicken wings and cook for about 2-3 minutes.
7) Press "Cancel" and place the reserved marinade over wings evenly.

8) Cover the pot with "Pressure Lid" and seal it.
9) Press "Pressure" and set the time for 7 minutes.
10) Press "Start" to begin cooking.
11) When cooking time is completed, do a "Quick" release.
12) Meanwhile, in a bowl, add the remaining ingredients and mix until well combined.
13) Open the lid and top the wings with sauce mixture.
14) Now, cover the pot with "Air Fryer Lid" and seal it.
15) Press "Broil" and set the time for 6 minutes.
16) Press "Start" to begin cooking.
17) When cooking time is completed, open the lid, and serve hot with the sprinkling of red pepper flakes.

Cod Nuggets

Prep time: 15 minutes | Cook time: 10 minutes | Serves: 6 | Program: Air Fry | Per Serving: Calories 270

Ingredients:

- All-purpose flour – 1 C.
- Eggs – 2
- Breadcrumbs – ¾ C.
- Pinch of salt
- Olive oil – 2 tbsp.
- Cod fillet – 1 lb. cut into 1x2½-inch strips

Directions:

1) In a shallow dish, place the flour.
2) Crack the eggs in a second dish and beat well.
3) In a third dish, mix together the breadcrumbs, salt, and oil.
4) Coat the nuggets with flour, then dip into beaten eggs and finally coat with the breadcrumbs.
5) Arrange the greased Air Fryer Basket in the bottom of Instant Pot Duo Crisp.
6) Cover the pot with "Air Fryer Lid" and seal it.
7) Press "Air Fry" and set the temperature to 320 °F for 10 minutes.
8) Press "Start" to begin preheating.
9) When the unit shows "Hot" instead of "On", open the lid and place the nuggets into the basket.
10) Again, seal the lid and press "Start" to begin cooking.
11) When cooking time is completed, open the lid, and serve warm.

Mushroom Pâté

Prep time: 15 minutes | Cook time: 30 minutes | Serves: 6 | Program: Pressure | Per Serving: Calories 122

Ingredients:

- Boiling water – 1 C.
- Dry porcini mushrooms – ¾ C. rinsed
- Unsalted butter – 2 tbsp.

- Yellow onion – 1 small, sliced
- Fresh cremini mushrooms – 1 lb. sliced thinly
- Chicken broth – 2-3 tbsp.
- Fresh lemon juice – 1 tbsp.
- Bay leaf – 1
- Salt and ground white pepper, as required
- Olive oil – 1 tbsp.
- Parmigiano-Reggiano cheese – 3 tbsp. grated

Directions:

1) In a heat-proof bowl, mix together boiling water and dry porcini mushrooms.
2) Cover the bowl tightly and set aside.
3) In the pot of Instant Pot Duo Crisp, place the butter and press "Sauté".
4) Press "Start" to begin cooking and heat for about 2-3 minutes.
5) Now add the onion and cook for about 5 minutes.
6) Add the fresh mushrooms and cook for about 5 minutes.
7) Add broth and lemon juice and cook for about 5 minutes or until all the liquid is absorbed.
8) Press "Cancel" to stop cooking and stir in porcini mushrooms with soaking liquid, bay leaf, salt, and white pepper.
9) Cover the pot with "Pressure Lid" and seal it.
10) Press "Pressure" and set the time for 12 minutes.
11) Press "Start" to begin cooking.
12) When cooking time is completed, do a "Natural" release.
13) Open the lid and discard the bay leaf.
14) Stir in the olive oil and with an immersion blender, blend the mixture until smooth.
15) Add the cheese and blend until well combined.

16) Transfer the mixture into a bowl and refrigerate for about 2 hours before serving.

Baba Ghanoush

Prep time: 15 minutes | Cook time: 2 hours | Serves: 6 | Program: Slow Cook | Per Serving: Calories 31

Ingredients:

- Medium eggplant – 1, peeled and chopped
- Garlic clove – 1, minced
- Fresh lemon juice – 3 tbsp.
- Tahini – 1 tbsp.
- Liquid smoke – ¼ tsp.
- Salt and ground black pepper, as required
- Extra-virgin olive oil – ½ tsp.

Directions:

1) In the pot of Instant Pot Duo Crisp, place the eggplant, garlic, lemon juice, tahini, liquid smoke, salt, and black pepper and mix well.
2) Cover the pot with "Air Fryer Lid" and seal it.
3) Press "Slow Cook" and set the time for 2 hours.
4) Press "Start" to begin cooking.

5) When cooking time is completed, open the lid and with a potato masher, mash until desired consistency is achieved.
6) Transfer the mixture into a bowl and drizzle with oil.
7) Serve warm.

Cheese Dip

Prep time: 10 minutes | Cook time: 50 minutes | Serves: 12 | Program: Bake | Per Serving: Calories 78

Ingredients:

- Yellow onion – 2/3 C. chopped
- Cheddar cheese – 1 C. shredded
- Swiss cheese – ½ C. shredded
- Parmesan cheese – ¼ C. shredded
- Whipped salad dressing – 2/3 C.
- Unsweetened almond milk – ½ C.
- Salt, as required

Directions:

1) In a large bowl, add all the ingredients and mix well.
2) Transfer the mixture into a baking dish and spread in an even layer.
3) Arrange the Multi-Functional Rack in the pot of Instant Pot Duo Crisp.

4) Cover the pot with "Air Fryer Lid" and seal it.
5) Press "Bake" and set the temperature to 375 °F for 50 minutes.
6) Press "Start" to begin preheating.
7) When the unit shows "Hot" instead of "On", open the lid and place the baking dish over the rack.
8) Again, seal the lid and press "Start" to begin cooking.
9) When cooking time is completed, open the lid, and serve hot.

Beef Dip

Prep time: 15 minutes | Cook time: 2 hours 10 minutes | Serves: 20 |
Program: Slow Cook | Per Serving: Calories 188

Ingredients:

- Lean ground beef – 2 lb.
- Yellow onion – 1 C. chopped
- Garlic cloves – 2, minced
- Mild chili peppers – 1 (4-oz.) can, chopped
- Tomato sauce – 2 (6-oz.) cans
- Cream cheese – 16 oz. Cubed
- Parmesan cheese – ½ C. grated
- Ketchup – ½ C.
- Dried oregano – 1 tsp.
- Red chili powder – 1½ tsp.

- Ground cumin – ½ tsp.
- Salt and ground black pepper, as required

Directions:

1) Press "Sauté" on the Instant Pot Duo Crisp and preheat for about 3-5 minutes.
2) Add the beef and cook for about 4-5 minutes.
3) Press "Cancel" to stop cooking and with a slotted spoon, remove the grease from the pot.
4) Add the remaining ingredients and stir to combine.
5) Cover the pot with "Air Fryer Lid" and seal it.
6) Press "Slow Cook" and set the time for 2 hours.
7) Press "Start" to begin cooking.
8) When cooking time is completed, open the lid, and serve hot.

Vegetarian Recipes

Simple Asparagus

Prep time: 10 minutes | Cook time: 2 minutes | Serves: 4 | Program: Steam | Per Serving: Calories 83

Ingredients:

- Fresh asparagus – 1 lb. trimmed
- Olive oil – 2 tbsp.
- Salt and ground black pepper, as required

Directions:

1) In the pot of Instant Pot Duo Crisp, place 1 C. of water.
2) Arrange the Multi-Functional Rack in the pot.
3) Place the asparagus over the rack.
4) Cover the pot with "Pressure Lid" and seal it.
5) Press "Steam" and set the time for 2 minutes.
6) Press "Start" to begin cooking.
7) When cooking time is completed, do a "Quick" release.
8) Open the lid and transfer the asparagus onto serving plates.
9) Drizzle with oil and sprinkle with salt and black pepper.
10) Serve hot.

Jacket Potatoes

Prep time: 15 minutes | Cook time: 20 minutes | Serves: 2 | Program: Air Fry | Per Serving: Calories 227

Ingredients:

- Potatoes – 2
- Mozzarella cheese – 1 tbsp. shredded
- Sour cream – 3 tbsp.
- Butter – 1 tbsp. softened
- Fresh chives – 1 tsp. chopped
- Salt and ground black pepper, as required

Directions:

1) With a fork, prick the potatoes.
2) Arrange the greased Air Fryer Basket in the pot of Instant Pot Duo Crisp.
3) Cover the pot with "Air Fryer Lid" and seal it.
4) Press "Air Fry" and set the temperature to 355 °F for 20 minutes.
5) Press "Start" to begin preheating.
6) When the unit shows "Hot" instead of "On", open the lid and place the potatoes into the basket.
7) Again, seal the lid and press "Start" to begin cooking.
8) When cooking time is completed, open the lid, and transfer the potatoes onto a platter.

9) In a bowl, add the remaining ingredients and mix until well combined.
10) Open potatoes from the center and stuff them with cheese mixture.
11) Serve immediately.

Stuffed Tomatoes

Prep time: 10 minutes | Cook time: 15 minutes | Serves: 2 | Program: Air Fry | Per Serving: Calories 206

Ingredients:

- Large tomatoes – 2
- Broccoli – ½ C. chopped finely
- Cheddar cheese – ½ C. Shredded
- Salt and ground black pepper, as required
- Unsalted butter – 1 tbsp. melted
- Dried thyme – ½ tsp. crushed

Directions:

1) Carefully, cut the top of each tomato and scoop out pulp and seeds.
2) In a bowl, mix together chopped broccoli, cheese, salt, and black pepper.
3) Stuff each tomato with broccoli mixture evenly.
4) Arrange the greased Air Fryer Basket in the pot of Instant Pot Duo Crisp.

5) Cover the pot with "Air Fryer Lid" and seal it.
6) Press "Air Fry" and set the temperature to 355 °F for 15 minutes.
7) Press "Start" to begin preheating.
8) When the unit shows "Hot" instead of "On", open the lid and place the tomatoes into the basket.
9) Again, seal the lid and press "Start" to begin cooking.
10) When cooking time is completed, open the lid and transfer the tomatoes onto a platter.
11) Serve with the garnishing of thyme.

Garlicky Brussels Sprout

Prep time: 10 minutes | Cook time: 1 hour 6 minutes | Serves: 3 |
Program: Sous Vide | Per Serving: Calories 108

Ingredients:

- Olive oil – 1 tbsp.
- Garlic cloves – 2, minced
- Salt and ground black pepper, as required

- Brussels sprouts – 1 lb. trimmed

Directions:

1) Fill the pot of Instant Pot Duo Crisp with water up to ½-full mark .
2) Press "Sous Vide" and set the temperature to 180 °F for 1 hour.

3) Cover the pot with "Pressure Lid" and press "Start " to preheat.
4) Meanwhile, in a bowl, add all ingredients except for Brussels sprouts and mix until well combined.
5) In a cooking pouch, place Brussels sprouts and oil mixture. Seal the pouch tightly after squeezing out the excess air.
6) When the unit shows "Hot" instead of "On", open the lid and place the pouch in the pot.
7) Again, seal the lid and press "Start" to begin cooking.
8) When the cooking time is completed, open the lid, and remove the pouch from inner pot.
9) Carefully open the pouch and serve immediately.

Glazed Carrots

Prep time: 10 minutes | Cook time: 12 minutes | Serves: 4 | Program: Air Fry | Per Serving: Calories 77

Ingredients:

- Carrots – 3 C. peeled and cut into large chunks
- Olive oil – 1 tbsp.
- Maple syrup – 1 tbsp.
- Fresh parsley – 1 tbsp. minced
- Salt and ground black pepper, as required

Directions:

1) In a bowl, add the carrot, oil, maple syrup, thyme, salt, and black pepper.
2) Arrange the greased Air Fryer Basket in the bottom of the Instant Pot Duo Crisp.
3) Cover the pot with "Air Fryer Lid" and seal it. Press "Air Fry".
4) Set the temperature to 390 °F for 12 minutes.
5) Press "Start" to begin preheating.
6) When the unit shows "Hot" instead of "On", open the lid and place the carrot chunks into the basket.
7) Close the lid and Press "Start" to begin cooking.
8) While cooking, flip the carrot chunks once halfway through.
9) When cooking time is completed, open the lid, and serve hot.

Glazed Zucchini

Prep time: 10 minutes | Cook time: 20 minutes | Serves: 5 | Program: Air Fry | Per Serving: Calories 213

Ingredients:

- Zucchinis – 4 large, chopped
- Olive oil – 6 tbsp. divided
- Honey – 2 tbsp.
- Dijon mustard – 1 tsp.
- Dried herbs – 1 tsp.

- Garlic paste – 1 tsp.
- Salt, as required

Directions:

1) In a parchment paper-lined baking pan, place the zucchini and drizzle with 3 tbsp. of oil.
2) Arrange the Multi-Functional Rack in the pot of Instant Pot Duo Crisp.
3) Cover the pot with "Air Fryer Lid" and seal it.
4) Press "Air Fry" and set the temperature to 350 °F for 15 minutes.
5) Press "Start" to begin preheating.
6) When the unit shows "Hot" instead of "On", open the lid and place the baking pan on top of rack.
7) Again, seal the lid and press "Start" to begin cooking.
8) Meanwhile, in a bowl, add the remaining oil, honey, mustard, herbs, garlic, salt, and black pepper and mix well.
9) After 15 minutes of cooking, add the honey mixture into vegetable mixture and mix well.
10) Now, set the temperature to 392 °F for 5 minutes.
11) When cooking time is completed, open the lid, and serve immediately.

Creamy Mushrooms

Prep time: 15 minutes | Cook time: 25 minutes | Serves: 4 | Program: Pressure | Per Serving: Calories 90

Ingredients:

- Fresh mushrooms – 2½ C. sliced
- Unsweetened coconut milk – ½ C.
- Plain Greek yogurt – ¼ C.
- Fresh ginger – ¾ tsp. grated
- Salt and ground black pepper, as required

Directions:

1) In a Pyrex dish, mix together all the ingredients.
2) With a piece of foil, cover the dish.
3) In the pot of Instant Pot Duo Crisp, place 1 C. of water.
4) Arrange the Multi-Functional Rack in the pot.
5) Place the Pyrex dish over the rack.
6) Cover the pot with "Pressure Lid" and seal it.
7) Press "Pressure" and set the time for 25 minutes.
8) Press "Start" to begin cooking.
9) When cooking time is completed, do a "Natural" release.
10) Open the lid and stir the mixture well.
11) Serve hot.

Cauliflower with Capers

Prep time: 10 minutes | Cook time: 13 minutes | Serves: 4 | Program: Pressure/ Air Fry | Per Serving: Calories 167

Ingredients:

- Medium cauliflower head – 1
- Water – ½ C.
- Olive oil – ¼ C.
- Garlic cloves – 4, minced
- Capers – 2 tbsp. minced
- Red pepper flakes – 1 tsp. crushed
- Parmesan cheese – ½ C. grated

Directions:

1) With a knife, cut an X into the cauliflower head, slicing about halfway down.
2) In the pot of Instant Pot Duo Crisp, place ½ C. of water.
3) Place the cauliflower head into the Air Fryer Basket.
4) Arrange the basket in the pot.
5) Cover the pot with "Pressure Lid" and seal it.
6) Press "Pressure" and set the time for 3 minutes.
7) Press "Start" to begin cooking.
8) When cooking time is completed, do a "Quick" release.
9) Meanwhile, in a small bowl, add the oil, garlic, capers, and red pepper flakes and mix well.

42

10) Open the lid and place the oil mixture over the cauliflower evenly.
11) Sprinkle with Parmesan cheese.
12) Now, cover the pot with "Air Fryer Lid" and seal it.
13) Press "Air Fry" and set the temperature to 390 °F for 5 minutes.
14) Press "Start" to begin cooking.
15) When cooking time is completed, open the lid, and serve hot.

Spinach with Cottage Cheese

Prep time: 15 minutes | Cook time: 13 minutes | Serves: 6 | Program: Pressure | Per Serving: Calories 100

Ingredients:

- Butter – 1 tbsp.
- Large yellow onion – 1, chopped
- Garlic cloves – 4, minced
- Fresh ginger – 1 (1-inch) piece, minced
- Green chilies – 2, chopped
- Ground cumin – 1 tsp.
- Ground coriander – 1 tsp.
- Red chili powder – ½ tsp.
- Ground turmeric – ½ tsp.
- Salt, as required

- Fresh spinach – 20 oz. chopped
- Arrowroot flour – 2 tbsp.
- Cottage cheese – 10 oz. cut into small pieces

Directions:

1) In the pot of Instant Pot Duo Crisp, place the butter and press "Sauté".
2) Press "Start" to begin cooking and heat for about 2-3 minutes.
3) Now add the onion, garlic, ginger, green chili, and spices and cook for about 1 minute.
4) Add the spinach and cook for about 2 minutes.
5) Press "Cancel" to stop cooking and stir the mixture well.
6) Cover the pot with "Pressure Lid" and seal it.
7) Press "Pressure" and set the time for 4 minutes.
8) Press "Start" to begin cooking.
9) When cooking time is completed, do a "Natural" release.
10) Open the lid and with an immersion blender, blend the mixture until smooth.
11) Press "Sauté" of pot and place the cottage cheese into the spinach mixture.
12) Press "Start" to begin cooking and cook for about 2-3 minutes.
13) Press "Cancel" to stop cooking and serve hot.

Ratatouille

Prep time: 20 minutes | Cook time: 6 minutes | Serves: 5 | Program: Pressure | Per Serving: Calories 96

Ingredients:

- Large zucchini – 1, sliced into thin circles
- Medium eggplant – 1, sliced into thin circles
- Medium tomatoes – 2, sliced into thin circles
- Large red onion – 1, sliced into thin circles
- Fresh thyme leaves – 1 tbsp. minced and divided
- Salt and ground black pepper, as required
- Large garlic cloves – 2, chopped finely
- Olive oil – 2 tbsp.
- Balsamic vinegar – 1 tbsp.

Directions:

1) In a bowl, add all vegetables, half of thyme, salt and black pepper and toss to coat well.
2) In the bottom of a foil-lined springform pan, spread some of garlic.
3) Arrange alternating slices of zucchini, eggplant, tomatoes, and onion, starting at the outer edge of the pan towards the center, overlapping the slices slightly.
4) Sprinkle with the remaining garlic, thyme, salt, and black pepper.

5) Drizzle with oil and vinegar evenly.
6) In the pot of Instant Pot Duo Crisp, place 1 C. of water.
7) Arrange the Multi-Functional Rack in the pot.
8) Place springform pan over the rack.
9) Cover the pot with "Pressure Lid" and seal it.
10) Press "Pressure" and set the time for 6 minutes.
11) Press "Start" to begin cooking.
12) When cooking time is completed, do a "Natural" release.
13) Open the lid and serve hot.

Green Beans & Mushroom Casserole

Prep time: 15 minutes | Cook time: 12 minutes | Serves: 6 | Program: Air Fry | Per Serving: Calories 125

Ingredients:

- Fresh green beans – 24 oz. Trimmed
- Fresh button mushrooms – 2 C. sliced
- Olive oil – 3 tbsp.
- Fresh lemon juice – 2 tbsp.
- Ground sage – 1 tsp.
- Garlic powder – 1 tsp.
- Onion powder – 1 tsp.
- Salt and ground black pepper, as required
- French fried onions – 1/3 C.

Directions:

1) In a bowl, add the green beans, mushrooms, oil, lemon juice, sage, and spices and toss to coat well.
2) Arrange the greased Air Fryer Basket in the pot of Instant Pot Duo Crisp.
3) Cover the pot with "Air Fryer Lid" and seal it.
4) Press "Air Fry" and set the temperature to 400 °F for 12 minutes.
5) Press "Start" to begin preheating.
6) When the unit shows "Hot" instead of "On", open the lid and place the mushroom mixture into the basket.
7) Again, seal the lid and press "Start" to begin cooking.
8) While cooking, stir the mushroom mixture once halfway through.
9) When cooking time is completed, open the lid, and transfer the mushroom mixture into a serving dish.
10) Top with fried onions and serve.

Veggie Casserole

Prep time: 15 minutes | Cook time: 4½ hours | Serves: 6 | Program: Slow Cook | Per Serving: Calories 89

Ingredients:

- Unsalted butter – 1 tbsp. melted
- Medium zucchinis – 4, peeled and sliced in rounds
- Green bell pepper – 1, seeded and sliced into strips
- Tomatoes – 2 C. chopped finely

47

- White onion – 1, sliced thinly
- Fresh thyme – 1 tbsp. minced
- Fresh rosemary – 1 tbsp. minced
- Salt and ground black pepper, as required
- Parmesan cheese – ½ C. grated

Directions:

1) In the pot of Instant Pot Duo Crisp, add all ingredients except for cheese and mix well.
2) Cover the pot with "Air Fryer Lid" and seal it.
3) Press "Slow Cook" and set the time for 3 hours.
4) Press "Start" to begin cooking.
5) When cooking time is completed, open the lid, and sprinkle the top with the cheese evenly.
6) Again, cover the pot with "Air Fryer Lid" and seal it.
7) Press "Slow Cook" and set the time for 1½ hours.
8) Press "Start" to begin cooking.
9) When cooking time is completed, open the lid, and serve hot.

Marinated Tofu

Prep time: 15 minutes | Cook time: 25 minutes | Serves: 4 | Program: Air Fry | Per Serving: Calories 103

Ingredients:

- Soy sauce – 2 tbsp.

- Fish sauce – 2 tbsp.
- Olive oil – 1 tsp.
- Extra-firm tofu – 12 oz. drained and cubed into 1-inch size
- Unsalted butter – 1 tsp. melted

Directions:

1) In a large bowl, add the soy sauce, fish sauce and oil and mix until well combined.
2) Add the tofu cubes and toss to coat well.
3) Set aside to marinate for about 30 minutes, tossing occasionally.
4) Arrange the greased Air Fryer Basket in the pot of Instant Pot Duo Crisp.
5) Cover the pot with "Air Fryer Lid" and seal it.
6) Press "Air Fry" and set the temperature to 355 °F for 25 minutes.
7) Press "Start" to begin preheating.
8) When the unit shows "Hot" instead of "On", open the lid and place the tofu cubes into the basket.
9) Again, seal the lid and press "Start" to begin cooking.
10) Flip the tofu after every 10 minutes during the cooking.
11) When cooking time is completed, open the lid, and serve hot.

Onion Soup

Prep time: 15 minutes | Cook time: 5 hours 13 minutes | Serves: 6 |
Program: Slow Cook | Per Serving: Calories 105

Ingredients:

- Olive oil – 2 tbsp.
- Medium sweet onions – 2, sliced.
- Garlic cloves – 2, minced
- Low-sodium soy sauce – ¼ C.
- Unsweetened applesauce – 1 tsp.
- Dried oregano – 1 tsp. crushed
- Dried basil – 1 tsp. crushed
- Ground black pepper, as required
- Vegetable broth – 5 C.
- Parmesan cheese – ¼ C. grated

Directions:

1) In the pot of Instant Pot Duo Crisp, place the oil and press "Sauté".
2) Press "Start" to begin cooking and heat for about 2-3 minutes.
3) Now add the onion and cook for about 8-9 minutes.
4) Add the garlic and cook for about 1 minute.
5) Press "Cancel" to stop cooking and stir in the remaining ingredients except for cheese.

6) Cover the pot with "Air Fryer Lid" and seal it.
7) Press "Slow Cook" and set the time for 5 hours.
8) Press "Start" to begin cooking.
9) When cooking time is completed, open the lid, and stir in the cheese until melted completely.
10) Serve hot.

Tomato Soup

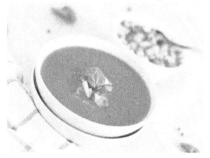

Prep time: 10 minutes | Cook time: 20 minutes | Serves: 4 | Program: Sous Vide | Per Serving: Calories 250

Ingredients:

- Fresh tomatoes – 4 C. cored and halved
- Onion – ½, chopped
- Fresh basil – 1/3 C. chopped and divided
- Garlic cloves – 2, minced
- Salt and ground black pepper, as required
- Extra-virgin olive oil – 5 tbsp.
- Crème fraiche – 5 tbsp.

Directions:

1) Fill the pot of Instant Pot Duo Crisp with water up to ½-full mark .
2) Press "Sous Vide" and set the temperature to 176 °F for 20 minutes.

3) Cover the pot with "Pressure Lid" and press "Start " to preheat.
4) Meanwhile, in a cooking pouch, place the tomatoes, onion, ¼ C. of basil and garlic.
5) Seal the pouch tightly after squeezing out the excess air.
6) When the unit shows "Hot" instead of "On", open the lid and place the pouch in the pot.
7) Again, seal the lid and press "Start" to begin cooking.
8) When the cooking time is completed, open the lid, and remove the pouch from inner pot.
9) Carefully open the pouch and transfer the tomato mixture into a blender.
10) Add olive oil, crème fraiche, salt and pepper and pulse until smooth.
10) Serve immediately with the garnishing of remaining basil.

Lentil Soup

Prep time: 15 minutes | Cook time: 9 hours 10 minutes | Serves: 12 |
Program: Slow Cook | Per Serving: Calories 179

Ingredients:

- Olive oil – 2 tbsp.
- Onions – 3 C. chopped finely
- Celery stalks – 3 C. chopped finely
- Garlic cloves – 4, minced

- Ground coriander – 1 tsp.
- Ground cumin – 1 tsp.
- Ground turmeric – 1 tsp.
- Ground cinnamon – ¼ tsp.
- Ground black pepper, as required
- Cauliflower – 3 C. chopped
- Diced tomatoes – 1 (28-oz.) can
- Lentils – 1¾ C. rinsed
- Tomato paste – 2 tbsp.
- Vegetable broth – 6 C.
- Water – 2 C.
- Fresh spinach – 4 C. chopped
- Fresh cilantro – ½ C. chopped

Directions:

1) In the pot of Instant Pot Duo Crisp, place the oil and press "Sauté".
2) Press "Start" to begin cooking and heat for about 2-3 minutes.
3) Now add the onion and celery and cook for about 4-6 minutes.
4) Add the garlic and spices and cook for about 1 minute.
5) Press "Cancel" to stop cooking and stir in the remaining ingredients except for spinach and cilantro.
6) Cover the pot with "Air Fryer Lid" and seal it.
7) Press "Slow Cook" and set the time for 8½ hours.
8) Press "Start" to begin cooking.
9) When cooking time is completed, open the lid, and stir in the spinach.
10) Again, cover the pot with "Air Fryer Lid" and seal it.
11) Press "Slow Cook" and set the time for 30 minutes.
12) Press "Start" to begin cooking.

13) When cooking time is completed, open the lid, and serve hot with the garnishing of cilantro.

Lentil Chili

Prep time: 15 minutes | Cook time: 22 minutes | Serves: 7 | Program: Pressure | Per Serving: Calories 318

Ingredients:

- Olive oil – 1 tbsp.
- Carrots – 2, peeled and chopped
- Onion – 1, chopped
- Garlic cloves – 4, minced
- Jalapeño peppers – 2, chopped
- Ground cumin – 1 tbsp.
- Ground coriander – ½ tsp.
- Dried oregano – 1 tsp.
- Salt, as required
- Fire-roasted diced tomatoes – 1 (28-oz.) can
- Crushed tomatoes – 1 (15-oz.) can
- Green lentils – 2 C.
- Vegetable broth – 4 C.
- Fresh lime juice – 1 tsp.

Directions:

1) In the pot of Instant Pot Duo Crisp, place the oil and press "Sauté".
2) Press "Start" to begin cooking and heat for about 2-3 minutes.
3) Now add the carrots, onion, garlic, and jalapeño peppers and cook for about 3-4 minutes.
4) Press "Cancel" to stop cooking and stir in the remaining ingredients.
5) Cover the pot with "Pressure Lid" and seal it.
6) Press "Pressure" and set the time for 15 minutes.
7) Press "Start" to begin cooking.
8) When cooking time is completed, do a "Quick" release.
9) Open the lid and stir in lime juice.
10) Serve hot.

Beans, Corn & Quinoa Chili

Prep time: 15 minutes │ Cook time: 6 hours 10 minutes │ Serves: 6 │ Program: Slow Cook │ Per Serving: Calories 387

Ingredients:

- Olive oil – 2 tsp.
- Large yellow onion – 1, chopped
- Celery stalks – 2, chopped
- Garlic cloves – 3, chopped
- Water – ¼ C.
- Tomato paste – 2 tbsp.

- Chipotle in adobo – 1½ tbsp. chopped finely
- Red chili powder – 2 tsp.
- Ground coriander – 1 tsp.
- Ground cumin – 1 tsp.
- Ground cinnamon – ½ tsp.
- Smoked paprika – ½ tsp.
- Pinch of cayenne pepper
- Vegetable broth – 3 C.
- Cooked black beans – 4 C.
- Corn – 2 C.
- Uncooked quinoa – 1 C. rinsed
- Fire-roasted diced tomatoes with juice – 1 (15-oz.) can

Directions:

1) In the pot of Instant Pot Duo Crisp, place the oil and press "Sauté".
2) Press "Start" to begin cooking and heat for about 2-3 minutes.
3) Now add the onion and celery and cook for about 5-6 minutes.
4) Add the garlic and cook for about 1 minute.
5) Add the water, tomato paste, chipotle and spices and cook for about 1 minute, stirring continuously.
6) Press "Cancel" to stop cooking and stir in the broth, black beans, quinoa and tomatoes with juice.
7) Cover the pot with "Air Fryer Lid" and seal it.
8) Press "Slow Cook" and set the time for 6 hours.
9) Press "Start" to begin cooking.
10) When cooking time is completed, open the lid, and serve hot.

Chickpeas Curry

Prep time: 15 minutes | Cook time: 29 minutes | Serves: 6 | Program: Pressure | Per Serving: Calories 164

Ingredients:

- Olive oil – 1 tbsp.
- Onion – 1, chopped
- Fresh ginger – 1 tbsp. minced
- Garlic – 1 tbsp. minced
- Curry powder – 1 tsp.
- Ground cumin – 1 tsp.
- Ground coriander – ½ tsp.
- Medium tomatoes – 2, chopped finely
- Dried chickpeas – 1 C. rinsed, soaked overnight and drained
- Water – 2 C.
- Salt and ground black pepper, as required
- Fresh cilantro – ¼ C. chopped

Directions:

1) In the pot of Instant Pot Duo Crisp, place the oil and press "Sauté".
2) Press "Start" to begin cooking and heat for about 2-3 minutes.
3) Now add the onion and cook for about 3 minutes.

4) Add the ginger, garlic and spices and cook for about 1 minute.
5) Add tomatoes and cook for about 2 minutes.
6) Press "Cancel" to stop cooking and stir in the chickpeas and water.
7) Cover the pot with "Pressure Lid" and seal it.
8) Press "Pressure" and set the time for 20 minutes.
9) Press "Start" to begin cooking.
10) When cooking time is completed, do a "Quick" release.
11) Open the lid and stir in the salt, black pepper, and cilantro.
12) Serve hot.

Asparagus Risotto

Prep time: 15 minutes | Cook time: 15 minutes | Serves: 8 | Program: Pressure | Per Serving: Calories 267

Ingredients:

- Unsalted butter – 2 tbsp.
- Onion – 2 C. chopped finely
- Arborio rice – 2 C.
- Fresh asparagus – 1½ C. tough ends removed and cut into 1-inch chunks
- Cherry tomatoes – 1 C.
- Garlic cloves – 3, minced
- Low-sodium chicken broth – 3 C.

- Fresh lemon juice – 2 tbsp.
- Dried oregano – 1 tsp.
- Salt, as required
- Parmesan cheese – 2/3 C. shredded

Directions:

1) In the pot of Instant Pot Duo Crisp, place the butter and press "Sauté".
2) Press "Start" to begin cooking and heat for about 2-3 minutes.
3) Now add the onion and cook for about 3 minutes.
4) Stir in the rice and cook for about 3 minutes.
5) Press "Cancel" to stop cooking and stir in the veggies, broth, lemon juice, oregano, and salt.
6) Cover the pot with "Pressure Lid" and seal it.
7) Press "Pressure" and set the time for 6 minutes.
8) Press "Start" to begin cooking.
9) When cooking time is completed, do a "Quick" release.
10) Open the lid and stir in the Parmesan cheese.
11) Serve warm.

Poultry Recipes

Herbed Whole Chicken

Prep time: 15 minutes | Cook time: 32 minutes | Serves: 6 | Program:
Pressure/ Air Fry | Per Serving: Calories 658

Ingredients:

- Dried basil – 1 tsp.
- Dried rosemary – 1 tsp.
- Garlic salt – 1 tsp.
- Seasoned salt – ½ tsp.
- Whole chicken – 1 (4½-lb.), neck and giblets removed
- Low-sodium chicken broth – 1½ C.
- Olive oil cooking spray

Directions:

1) In a bowl, mix together the basil, rosemary, garlic salt and seasoned salt.
2) Season the chicken with herb mixture evenly.
3) In the pot of Instant Pot Duo Crisp, pour the chicken broth.
4) Arrange the Multi-Functional Rack in the bottom of pot.
5) Arrange the chicken over the rack.

6) Cover the pot with "Pressure Lid" and seal it.
7) Press "Pressure" and set the time for 22 minutes.
8) Press "Start" to begin cooking.
9) When cooking time is completed, do a "Quick" release.
10) Open the lid and spray the chicken with cooking spray.
11) Now cover the pot with "Air Fryer Lid" and seal it.
12) Press "Air Fry" and set the temperature to 400 °F for 10 minutes.
13) Press "Start" to begin preheating.
14) When cooking time is completed, open the lid, and place the chicken onto a platter for about 10 minutes before carving.
15) Cut into desired sized pieces and serve.

Spiced Pulled Chicken

Prep time: 15 minutes | Cook time: 8 hours | Serves: 4 | Program: Slow Cook | Per Serving: Calories 576

Ingredients:

- Boneless, skinless chicken breasts – 1 lb.
- Ground cumin – 1½ tsp.
- Red chili powder – 1 tsp.
- Salt and ground black pepper, as required
- Chicken broth – 1½ C.

Directions:

1) In the pot of Instant Pot Duo Crisp, add all ingredients and mix well.
2) Cover the pot with "Air Fryer Lid" and seal it.
3) Press "Slow Cook" and set the time for 8 hours.
4) Press "Start" to begin cooking.
5) When cooking time is completed, open the lid, and transfer the breasts into a large bowl.
6) With a fork, shred the meat.
7) Top with some cooking liquid and serve.

Spicy & Lemony Chicken Legs

Prep time: 10 minutes │ Cook time: 20 minutes │ Serves: 4 │ Program: Air Fry │ Per Serving: Calories 461

Ingredients:

- Chicken legs – 4 (8-oz.)
- Fresh lemon juice – 3 tbsp.
- Ginger paste – 3 tsp.
- Garlic paste – 3 tsp.
- Salt, as required
- Plain Greek yogurt – 4 tbsp.
- Garam masala powder – 2 tbsp.
- Red chili powder – 2 tsp.
- Ground cumin – 1 tsp.
- Ground coriander – 1 tsp.

- Ground turmeric – 1 tsp.
- Ground black pepper, as required

Directions:

1) In a bowl, add the chicken legs, lemon juice, ginger paste, garlic paste and salt and mix well. Set aside for about 15 minutes.
2) Meanwhile, in another bowl, mix together the yogurt and spices.
3) Add the chicken legs into the bowl and coat with the yogurt mixture generously.
4) Cover the bowl of chicken and refrigerate for at least 10-12 hours.
5) Arrange the greased Air Fryer Basket in the pot of Instant Pot Duo Crisp.
6) Cover the pot with "Air Fryer Lid" and seal it.
7) Press "Air Fry" and set the temperature to 445 °F for 20 minutes.
8) Press "Start" to begin preheating.
9) When the unit shows "Hot" instead of "On", open the lid and place the chicken legs into the basket.
10) Again, seal the lid and press "Start" to begin cooking.
11) When cooking time is completed, open the lid, and serve hot.

Sweet & Spicy Chicken Drumsticks

Prep time: 10 minutes | Cook time: 20 minutes | Serves: 4 | Program: Air Fry | Per Serving: Calories 343

Ingredients:

- Garlic clove – 1, crushed
- Cayenne pepper – 1 tsp.
- Red chili powder – 1 tsp.
- Sugar – 2 tsp.
- Mustard – 1 tbsp.
- Salt and ground black pepper, as required
- Olive oil – 1 tbsp.
- Chicken drumsticks – 4 (6-oz.)

Directions:

1) In a bowl, mix together all ingredients except for chicken drumsticks.
2) Rub the chicken with the oil mix and refrigerate to marinate for about 20-30 minutes.
3) Arrange the greased Air Fryer Basket in the bottom of Instant Pot Duo Crisp.
4) Cover the pot with "Air Fryer Lid" and seal it.
5) Press "Air Fry" and set the temperature to 390 °F for 10 minutes.
6) Press "Start" to begin preheating.

7) When the unit shows "Hot" instead of "On", open the lid and place the drumsticks into the basket.
8) Again, seal the lid and press "Start" to begin cooking.
9) After 10 minutes of cooking, set the temperature to 300 °F for 10 minutes.
10) When cooking time is completed, open the lid, and serve hot.

Rosemary Chicken Thighs

Prep time: 10 minutes | Cook time: 20 minutes | Serves: 2 | Program: Bake | Per Serving: Calories 246

Ingredients:

- Boneless, skinless chicken thighs – 2 (4-oz.)
- Fresh rosemary – 1 tsp. minced
- Salt and ground black pepper, as required
- Butter – 2 tbsp. melted

Directions:

1) Brush the chicken thighs with melted butter and then sprinkle with rosemary, salt and black pepper.
2) Place the chicken thighs into a greased baking dish.
3) Arrange the Multi-Functional Rack in the pot of Instant Pot Duo Crisp.
4) Cover the pot with "Air Fryer Lid" and seal it.

5) Press "Bake" and set the temperature to 450 °F for 20 minutes.
6) Press "Start" to begin preheating.
7) When the unit shows "Hot" instead of "On", open the lid and place the baking dish over the rack.
8) Again, seal the lid and press "Start" to begin cooking.
9) When cooking time is completed, open the lid, and serve hot.

Braised Chicken Thighs

Prep time: 10 minutes | Cook time: 28 minutes | Serves: 6 | Program: Pressure | Per Serving: Calories 333

Ingredients:

- Butter – 2 tbsp.
- Yellow onion – 1, chopped
- Chicken thighs – 2 lb.
- Chicken broth – ¾ C.
- Salt and ground black pepper, as required

Directions:

1) In the pot of Instant Pot Duo Crisp, place the butter and press "Sauté".
2) Press "Start" to begin cooking and heat for about 2-3 minutes.
3) Now add the onion and cook for about 5 minutes.

4) Press "Cancel" to stop cooking and stir in the remaining ingredients.
5) Cover the pot with "Pressure Lid" and seal it.
6) Press "Pressure" and set the time for 20 minutes.
7) Press "Start" to begin cooking.
8) When cooking time is completed, do a "Quick" release.
9) Open the lid and serve hot.

Mozzarella Chicken Breasts

Prep time: 10 minutes | Cook time: 12 minutes | Serves: 6 | Program: Pressure/ Air Fry | Per Serving: Calories 376

Ingredients:

- Medium onion – 1, sliced thinly
- Boneless, skinless chicken breasts – 6 (5-oz.)
- Salt, as required
- Italian seasoning – 1 tsp.
- Basil pesto – 5 oz.
- Mozzarella cheese – 6 oz. shredded
- Roma tomatoes – 3, sliced

Directions:

1) In the pot of Instant Pot Duo Crisp, place the onion slices and top with the chicken breasts in a single layer.

2) Sprinkle the chicken breasts with Italian seasonings and salt and top with the pesto sauce evenly.
3) Cover the pot with "Pressure Lid" and seal it.
4) Press "Pressure" and set the time for 4 minutes.
5) Press "Start" to begin cooking.
6) When cooking time is completed, do a "Natural" release for about 5 minutes, then do a "Quick" release.
7) Meanwhile, cut ¾ of mozzarella cheese into thin slices and grate the remaining.
8) Open the lid and stir the chicken with onion mixture.
9) Arrange the mozzarella slices on top of chicken, followed by tomato slices.
10) Now cover the pot with "Air Fryer Lid" and seal it.
11) Press "Air Fry" and set the temperature to 325 °F for 5 minutes.
12) Press "Start" to begin cooking.
13) When cooking time is completed, open the lid and immediately, sprinkle with grated cheese.
14) Immediately, cover with the lid for about 2-3 minutes before serving.

Spinach Stuffed Chicken Breasts

Prep time: 15 minutes | Cook time: 33 minutes | Serves: 2 | Program: Air Fry | Per Serving: Calories 279

Ingredients:

- Olive oil – 1 tbsp.
- Fresh spinach – 1¾ oz.
- Ricotta cheese – ¼ C. shredded
- Boneless, skinless chicken breasts – 2 (4-oz.)
- Salt and ground black pepper, as required
- Cheddar cheese – 2 tbsp. grated
- Paprika – ¼ tsp.

Directions:

1) In the pot of Instant Pot Duo Crisp, place the oil and press "Sauté".
2) Press "Start" to begin cooking and heat for about 2-3 minutes.
3) Now add the spinach and cook for about 3-4 minutes.
4) Stir in the ricotta and cook for about 40-60 seconds.
5) Press "Cancel" to stop cooking and transfer the spinach mixture into a bowl. Set aside to cool.
6) Cut slits into the chicken breasts about ¼-inch apart but not all the way through.
7) Stuff each chicken breast with the spinach mixture.
8) Sprinkle each chicken breast with salt and black pepper and then with cheddar cheese and paprika.
9) Arrange the greased Air Fryer Basket in the bottom of Instant Pot Duo Crisp.
10) Cover the pot with "Air Fryer Lid" and seal it.
11) Press "Air Fry" and set the temperature to 390 °F for 25 minutes.
12) Press "Start" to begin preheating.
13) When the unit shows "Hot" instead of "On", open the lid and place the chicken breasts into the basket.
14) Again, seal the lid and press "Start" to begin cooking.
15) When cooking time is completed, open the lid, and serve hot.

Butter Chicken

Prep time: 15 minutes | Cook time: 12 minutes | Serves: 8 | Program: Pressure | Per Serving: Calories 492

Ingredients:

- Butter – ½ C. cubed and divided
- Large yellow onion – 1, chopped finely
- Garlic cloves – 6, minced
- Fresh ginger – 2 tbsp. minced
- Boneless, skinless chicken breasts – 3 lb. cubed
- Tomato sauce – 1 C.
- Tomato paste – 3 tbsp.
- Garam masala powder – 1½ tbsp.
- Ground turmeric – 1 tsp.
- Salt, as required
- Chicken broth – 2/3 C.
- Heavy cream – 2/3 C.
- Fresh cilantro – ¼ C. chopped

Directions:

1) In the pot of Instant Pot Duo Crisp, place the 2 tbsp. of the butter and press "Sauté".
2) Press "Start" to begin cooking and heat for about 2-3 minutes.

3) Now add the onion, garlic and ginger and cook for about 2 minutes.
4) Press "Cancel" to stop cooking and stir in the remaining ingredients except the cream and cilantro.
5) Cover the pot with "Pressure Lid" and seal it.
6) Press "Pressure" and set the time for 5 minutes.
7) Press "Start" to begin cooking.
8) When cooking time is completed, do a "Quick" release.
9) Open the lid and press "Sauté" of pot.
10) Press "Start" to begin cooking.
11) Stir in the remaining butter and heavy cream and cook for about 2 minutes.
12) Press "Cancel" to stop cooking and serve hot with the garnishing of cilantro.

Chicken with Mushrooms

Prep time: 15 minutes | Cook time: 8 hours 13 minutes | Serves: 6 |
Program: Slow Cook | Per Serving: Calories 306

Ingredients:

- Olive oil – 1 tbsp.
- Boneless, skinless chicken breasts – 6
- Fresh button mushrooms – 4 C. sliced
- Chicken broth – 1 C.
- Salt and ground black pepper, as required

Directions:

1) In the pot of Instant Pot Duo Crisp, place the oil and press "Sauté".
2) Press "Start" to begin cooking and heat for about 2-3 minutes.
3) Now add the chicken breasts and cook for about 5 minutes per side.
4) Press "Cancel" to stop cooking and stir in the remaining ingredients.
5) Cover the pot with "Air Fryer Lid" and seal it.
6) Press "Slow Cook" and set the time for 8 hours.
7) Press "Start" to begin cooking.
8) When cooking time is completed, open the lid, and serve hot.

Chicken Casserole

Prep time: 15 minutes | Cook time: 9 minutes | Serves: 8 | Program: Pressure/ Air Fry | Per Serving: Calories 372

Ingredients:

- Cooked chicken, shredded – 3 C.
- Large onion – ½, chopped
- Carrot – ½ C. peeled and chopped
- Celery stalks – 2, chopped
- Frozen peas – ¼ C.

- Frozen broccoli florets – ¼ C.
- Chicken broth – 5 C.
- Garlic powder – 1 tsp.
- Salt and ground black pepper, as required
- Egg noodles – 12 oz.
- Cream of chicken and mushroom soup – 1 (10½-oz.) can
- Cheddar cheese – 1 C. shredded
- Sour cream – ¼ C.
- French onions – 1 (6-oz.) package

Directions:

1) In the pot of Instant Pot Duo Crisp, place the chicken, vegetables, garlic powder, salt and pepper and broth and stir to combine.
2) Place the egg noodles on top and lightly, press in the chicken mixture.
3) Cover the pot with "Pressure Lid" and seal it.
4) Press "Pressure" and set the time for 4 minutes.
5) Press "Start" to begin cooking.
6) When cooking time is completed, do a "Quick" release.
7) Open the lid and stir in the can of soup, cheese, sour cream and 1/3 of the French onions.
8) Spread the remaining French's onions on top evenly.
9) Now cover the pot with "Air Fryer Lid" and seal it.
10) Press "Air Fry" and set the temperature to 400 °F for 5 minutes.
11) Press "Start" to begin cooking.
12) When cooking time is completed, open the lid, and serve hot.

Spicy Whole Turkey

Prep time: 20 minutes | Cook time: 8 hours 5 minutes | Serves: 14 |
Program: Slow Cook/ Broil | Per Serving: Calories 403

Ingredients:

For Spice Rub:

- Dried thyme – 2 tsp. crushed
- Ground cumin – 2 tsp.
- Paprika – 2 tsp.
- Salt, as required
- Ground white pepper, as required
- Ground black pepper, as required

For Turkey:

- Whole turkey – 1 (8-lb.), neck and giblets removed
- Garlic cloves – 4, smashed
- Medium onion – ½, chopped
- Carrots – 2, peeled and cut into thirds
- Celery stalks – 2, cut into thirds
- Lemon – 1, quartered

Directions:

1) For spice rub: in a bowl, mix together all ingredients.
2) Fold back the wings of turkey.
3) Rub smashed garlic over outside of turkey evenly.

4) Rub inside and outside of turkey with spice rub generously.
5) Place lemon quarters in the cavity of turkey.
6) Tie the legs of turkey with kitchen twine.
7) In the pot of Instant Pot Duo Crisp, place the onion, carrots, celery and 3 garlic cloves.
8) Arrange turkey over vegetables.
9) Cover the pot with "Air Fryer Lid" and seal it.
10) Press "Slow Cook" and set the time for 8 hours.
11) Press "Start" to begin cooking.
12) When cooking time is completed, open the lid, and transfer the turkey and vegetables onto a platter.
13) Now, arrange the Broiling Tray in the pot.
14) Place the turkey onto the tray.
15) Now, cover the pot with "Air Fryer Lid" and seal it.
16) Press "Broil" and set the time for 5 minutes.
17) Press "Start" to begin cooking.
18) When cooking time is completed, open the lid, and place the turkey onto a platter for about 25-30 minutes before slicing.
19) Cut into desired sized pieces and serve alongside the vegetables.

Smoky Turkey Legs

Prep time: 10 minutes | Cook time: 8 hours | Serves: 6 | Program: Slow Cook | Per Serving: Calories 622

Ingredients:

- Turkey legs – 6
- Salt and ground black pepper, as required
- Tomato paste – ¾ C.
- Balsamic vinegar – 2 tbsp.
- Sugar – 2 tbsp.
- Garlic powder – ¼ tsp.
- Onion powder – ¼ tsp.
- Liquid smoke – 2-3 drops
- Olive oil cooking spray

Directions:

1) Season each turkey leg with salt and black pepper generously.
2) In a bowl, add the remaining ingredients and mix until well combined.
3) Grease the pot of Instant Pot Duo Crisp with the cooking spray generously.
4) In the prepared pot, place the turkey legs and top with sauce evenly.
5) Cover the pot with "Air Fryer Lid" and seal it.

6) Press "Slow Cook" and set the time for 8 hours.
7) Press "Start" to begin cooking.
8) When cooking time is completed, open the lid, and serve hot.

Lime Turkey Legs

Prep time: 10 minutes | Cook time: 30 minutes | Serves: 2 | Program: Air Fry | Per Serving: Calories 709

Ingredients:

- Garlic cloves – 2, minced
- Fresh rosemary – 1 tbsp. minced
- Fresh lime zest – 1 tsp. finely grated
- Olive oil – 2 tbsp.
- Fresh lime juice – 1 tbsp.
- Salt and ground black pepper, as required
- Turkey legs – 2

Directions:

1) In a bowl, mix together the garlic, rosemary, lime zest, oil, lime juice, salt, and black pepper.
2) Add the turkey legs and generously coat with marinade.
3) Refrigerate to marinate for about 6-8 hours.
4) Arrange the greased Air Fryer Basket in the bottom of Instant Pot Duo Crisp.

5) Cover the pot with "Air Fryer Lid" and seal it.
6) Press "Air Fry" and set the temperature to 350 °F for 30 minutes.
7) Press "Start" to begin preheating.
8) When the unit shows "Hot" instead of "On", open the lid and place the turkey legs into the basket.
9) Again, seal the lid and press "Start" to begin cooking.
10) Flip the turkey legs once halfway through.
11) When cooking time is completed, open the lid, and serve hot.

Glazed Turkey Breast

Prep time: 10 minutes | Cook time: 55 minutes | Serves: 10 | Program: Air Fry | Per Serving: Calories 252

Ingredients:

- Boneless turkey breast – 1 (5-lb.)
- Salt and ground black pepper, as required
- Honey – 3 tbsp.
- Dijon mustard – 2 tbsp.
- Butter – 1 tbsp. softened

Directions:

1) Season the turkey breast with salt and black pepper generously and spray with cooking spray.

2) Arrange the greased Air Fryer Basket in the bottom of Instant Pot Duo Crisp.
3) Cover the pot with "Air Fryer Lid" and seal it.
4) Press "Air Fry" and set the temperature to 350 °F for 55 minutes.
5) Press "Start" to begin preheating.
6) When the unit shows "Hot" instead of "On", open the lid and place the turkey breast into the basket.
7) Again, seal the lid and press "Start" to begin cooking.
8) Meanwhile, for glaze: in a bowl, mix together the honey, mustard, and butter.
9) While cooking, flip the turkey breast twice, first after 25 minutes and then after 37 minutes.
10) After 50 minutes of cooking, coat the turkey breast with the glaze.
11) When cooking time is completed, open the lid, and place the turkey onto a cutting board for about 5 minutes before slicing.
12) Cut into desired sized slices and serve.

Bacon-Wrapped Turkey Breast

Prep time: 10 minutes | Cook time: 4 hours | Serves: 4 | Program: Slow Cook | Per Serving: Calories 435

Ingredients:

- Boneless turkey breast – 1 lb. trimmed

- Thin-cut bacon slices – 8 oz.
- Olive oil cooking spray
- Tomatoes – 3, peeled and chopped
- Garlic powder – ½ tsp.
- Salt and ground black pepper, as required

Directions:

1) Wrap the turkey breast with bacon slices.
2) Grease the pot of Instant Pot Duo Crisp with cooking spray generously.
3) In the prepared pot, place the tomatoes, garlic powder, salt and black pepper and mix well.
4) Place the bacon-wrapped turkey breast over tomato mixture.
5) Cover the pot with "Air Fryer Lid" and seal it.
6) Press "Slow Cook" and set the time for 4 hours.
7) Press "Start" to begin cooking.
8) When cooking time is completed, open the lid, and place the turkey breast onto a cutting board for about 5-10 minutes before slicing.
9) Cut the turkey breast into desired sized slices and serve alongside the pan sauce.

Buttered Turkey Wings

Prep time: 10 minutes | Cook time: 26 minutes | Serves: 4 | Program: Air Fry | Per Serving: Calories 546

Ingredients:

- Turkey wings – 2 lb.
- Butter – 3 tbsp. melted
- Dried rosemary – 1 tsp.
- Salt and ground black pepper, as required

Directions:

1) In a large bowl, add the turkey wings, butter, rosemary, salt, and black pepper and mix well.
2) Arrange the greased Air Fryer Basket in the pot of Instant Pot Duo Crisp.
3) Cover the pot with "Air Fryer Lid" and seal it.
4) Press "Air Fry" and set the temperature to 380 °F for 26 minutes.
5) Press "Start" to begin preheating.
6) When the unit shows "Hot" instead of "On", open the lid and place the turkey wings into the basket.
7) Again, seal the lid and press "Start" to begin cooking.
8) When cooking time is completed, open the lid, and serve hot.

Turkey Meatballs in Tomato Sauce

Prep time: 10 minutes | Cook time: 25 minutes | Serves: 6 | Program: Pressure | Per Serving: Calories 173

Ingredients:

- Ground turkey – 1 lb.
- Egg – 1
- Dried rosemary – 1 tsp.
- Salt and ground black pepper, as required
- Tomato sauce – 1½ C.

Directions:

1) In a bowl, add all the ingredients except for tomato sauce and mix until well combined.
2) Make equal-sized meatballs from the mixture.
3) In the pot of Instant Pot Duo Crisp, place the meatballs and tomato sauce and gently stir to combine.
4) Cover the pot with "Pressure Lid" and seal it.
5) Press "Pressure" and set the time for 25 minutes.
6) Press "Start" to begin cooking.
7) When cooking time is completed, do a "Quick" release.
8) Open the lid and serve hot.

Rosemary Whole Duck

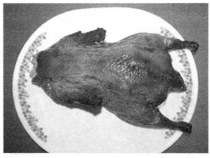

Prep time: 15 minutes | Cook time: 33 minutes | Serves: 5 | Program: Pressure | Per Serving: Calories 715

Ingredients:

- Wild duck – 1 (3½-lb.)
- Salt and ground black pepper, as required

- Butter – 2 tbsp.
- Lemon – 1, halved
- Fresh rosemary sprigs – 2
- Chicken broth – ½ C.

Directions:

1) With a fork, prick the skin of the duck.
2) Season the body and cavity of duck with salt and black pepper evenly.
3) Stuff the cavity of duck with lemon halves and rosemary sprigs and tie up the legs together.
4) In the pot of Instant Pot Duo Crisp, place the oil and press "Sauté".
5) Press "Start" to begin cooking and heat for about 2-3 minutes.
6) Now add the duck and cook for about 4-5 minutes or until browned from all sides.
7) Press "Cancel" to stop cooking and with a slotted spoon, remove the grease from pot.
8) Place the broth over duck.
9) Cover the pot with "Pressure Lid" and seal it.
10) Press "Pressure" and set the time for 25 minutes.
11) Press "Start" to begin cooking.
12) When cooking time is completed, do a "Natural" release.
13) Open the lid and place the duck onto a cutting board.
14) Cut into desired sized pieces and serve.

Buttered Duck Legs

Prep time: 10 minutes | Cook time: 6 hours | Serves: 4 | Program: Slow Cook | Per Serving: Calories 531

Ingredients:

- Butter – ¼ C. melted
- Duck legs – 4
- Salt and ground black pepper, as required

Directions:

1) Season the duck legs with salt and black pepper generously.
2) In a baking dish, arrange the duck legs in a single layer and refrigerate, covered overnight.
3) In the pot of Instant Pot Duo Crisp, place the melted butter.
4) Arrange the duck legs over melted butter in a single layer.
5) Cover the pot with "Air Fryer Lid" and seal it.
6) Press "Slow Cook" and set the time for 6 hours.
7) Press "Start" to begin cooking.
8) When cooking time is completed, open the lid, and serve hot.

Red Meat Recipes

Bacon-Wrapped Fillet Mignon

Prep time: 10 minutes | Cook time: 15 minutes | Serves: 2 | Program: Air Fry | Per Serving: Calories 465

Ingredients:

- Bacon slices – 2
- Filet mignon – 2 (6-oz.)
- Ground black pepper, as required
- Avocado oil – 1 tsp.

Directions:

1) Wrap 1 bacon slice around each filet and secure with a toothpick.
2) Season each filet evenly with black pepper and then, coat with avocado oil.
3) Arrange the greased Air Fryer Basket in the pot of Instant Pot Duo Crisp.
4) Cover the pot with "Air Fryer Lid" and seal it.
5) Press "Air Fry" and set the temperature to 375 °F for 15 minutes.
6) Press "Start" to begin preheating.

7) When the unit shows "Hot" instead of "On", open the lid and place the filets into the basket.
8) Again, seal the lid and press "Start" to begin cooking.
9) Flip the filets once halfway through.
10) When cooking time is completed, open the lid, and serve hot.

Spiced Skirt Steak

Prep time: 10 minutes | Cook time: 10 minutes | Serves: 4 | Program: Air Fry | Per Serving: Calories 522

Ingredients:

- Garlic cloves – 3, minced
- Fresh parsley leaves – ½ C. chopped finely
- Ground cumin – 1 tbsp.
- Smoked paprika – 3 tsp.
- Red pepper flakes – 1 tsp. crushed
- Salt and ground black pepper, as required
- Avocado oil – 2 tbsp.
- White wine vinegar – 2 tbsp.
- Skirt steaks – 2 (8-oz.)

Directions:

1) In a bowl, mix together all ingredients except the steaks.
2) In a resealable bag, add spice mixture and steaks.

3) Seal the bag tightly and shake to coat well.
4) Refrigerate for about 24 hours.
5) Remove steaks from the refrigerator and set aside at room temperature for about 30 minutes.
6) Arrange the greased Air Fryer Basket in the pot of Instant Pot Duo Crisp.
7) Cover the pot with "Air Fryer Lid" and seal it.
8) Press "Air Fry" and set the temperature to 390 °F for 20 minutes.
9) Press "Start" to begin preheating.
10) When the unit shows "Hot" instead of "On", open the lid and place the steaks into the basket.
11) Again, seal the lid and press "Start" to begin cooking.
12) When cooking time is completed, open the lid, and place the steaks onto a cutting board for about 5 minutes before slicing.
13) Cut the steaks into desired sized slices and serve.

Braised Chuck Roast

Prep time: 10 minutes | Cook time: 1 hour 19 minutes | Serves: 8 |
Program: Pressure | Per Serving: Calories 402

Ingredients:

- Coconut oil – 2 tbsp.
- Chuck roast – 3 lb. trimmed
- Salt, as required

- Medium onion – 1, sliced
- Water – 2 C.

Directions:

1) In the pot of Instant Pot Duo Crisp, place the oil and press "Sauté".
2) Press "Start" to begin cooking and heat for about 2-3 minutes.
3) Now add the roast and cook for about 2-3 minutes per side.
4) Press "Cancel" to stop cooking and sprinkle the roast with salt.
5) Top with onion, followed by the water.
6) Cover the pot with "Pressure Lid" and seal it.
7) Press "Pressure" and set the time for 70 minutes.
8) Press "Start" to begin cooking.
9) When cooking time is completed, do a "Natural" release.
10) Open the lid and place the roast onto a cutting board for about 10-15 minutes before slicing.
11) Cut into desired sized slices and serve.

Braised Beef Short Ribs

Prep time: 10 minutes | Cook time: 1 hour 8 minutes | Serves: 6 |
Program: Pressure/ Bake | Per Serving: Calories 523

Ingredients:

- Bone-in beef short ribs – 3 lb. trimmed, and silver skin removed
- Salt and ground black pepper, as required
- Olive oil – 2 tbsp.
- Sugar – 2 tbsp.
- Beef broth – ½ C.

Directions:

1) Rub the ribs with salt and black pepper evenly.
2) In the pot of Instant Pot Duo Crisp, place the oil and press "Sauté".
3) Press "Start" to begin cooking and heat for about 2-3 minutes.
4) Now add the ribs and cook for about 10 minutes.
5) Press "Cancel" to stop cooking and stir in the sugar, salt, black pepper, and broth.
6) Cover the pot with "Pressure Lid" and seal it.
7) Press "Pressure" and set the time for 40 minutes.
8) Press "Start" to begin cooking.
9) When cooking time is completed, do a "Quick" release.
10) Now, cover the pot with "Air Fryer Lid" and seal it.
11) Press "Bake" and set the temperature to 350 °F for 15 minutes.
12) Press "Start" to begin cooking.
13) Open the lid and serve hot.

Beef Jerky

Prep time: 10 minutes | Cook time: 7 hours | Serves: 6 | Program: Dehydrate | Per Serving: Calories 199

Ingredients:

- Low-sodium soy sauce – ¼ C.
- Worcestershire sauce – 2 tbsp.
- Brown sugar – 2 tbsp.
- Salt, as required
- Beef eye of round – 1½ lb. cut in ¼-inch slices

Directions:

1) In a bowl, add all the ingredients except beef and beat until sugar is dissolved.
2) In a large resealable plastic bag, place the beef slices and marinade.
3) Seal the bag and rub to coat.
4) Refrigerate to marinate overnight.
5) Remove from the refrigerator and strain the beef slices discarding the marinade.
6) Place the beef slices into the Dehydrating Tray in a single layer.
7) Arrange the tray in the pot of Instant Pot Duo Crisp.
8) Close the Instant Pot Duo Crisp with "Air Fryer Lid" and Select "Dehydrate".

9) Set the temperature to 155 °F for 7 hours.

10) Press "Start" to begin cooking.

11) When cooking time is completed, open the lid, and transfer the beef jerky onto a platter.

12) Set aside to cool before serving.

Lemony Flank Steak

Prep time: 10 minutes | Cook time: 12 minutes | Serves: 6 | Program: Broil | Per Serving: Calories 339

Ingredients:

- Flank steak – 2 lb.
- Fresh lemon juice – 3 tbsp.
- Olive oil – 2 tsp.
- Garlic cloves – 3, minced
- Red chili powder – 1 tsp.
- Salt and ground black pepper, as required

Directions:

1) In a large bowl, add all the ingredients except for steak and mix well.

2) Add the flank steak and coat with the marinade generously.

3) Refrigerate to marinate for 24 hours, flipping occasionally.

4) Arrange the greased Broiling Tray in the bottom of Instant Pot Duo Crisp.
5) Cover the pot with "Air Fryer Lid" and seal it.
6) Press "Broil" and set the time for 12 minutes.
7) Press "Start" to begin preheating.
8) When the unit shows "Hot" instead of "On", open the lid and place the steak onto the tray.
9) Again, seal the lid and press "Start" to begin cooking.
10) While cooking, flip the steak once halfway through.
11) When cooking time is completed, open the lid, and place the steak onto a cutting board for about 10-15 minutes before slicing.
12) With a sharp knife, cut the steak into desired sized slices and serve.

Beef Stew

Prep time: 15 minutes | Cook time: 7 hours 43 minutes | Serves: 6 |
Program: Slow Cook | Per Serving: Calories 407

Ingredients:

- Olive oil – 2 tbsp.
- Beef stew meat – 2 lb. cut into cubes
- Onions – 2, chopped
- Garlic cloves – 3-4, chopped finely
- Fresh ginger – 1 tsp. minced
- Dried thyme – 1 tsp. crushed

- Curry powder – 2 tbsp.
- Salt and ground black pepper, as required
- Beef broth – 4 C.
- Fresh lemon juice – 3 tbsp.
- Large carrots – 2, peeled and chopped
- Medium sweet potatoes – 2, peeled and cubed
- Fresh spinach – 3 C. torn

Directions:

1) In the pot of Instant Pot Duo Crisp, place the oil and press "Sauté".
2) Press "Start" to begin cooking and heat for about 2-3 minutes.
3) Now add the beef cubes and cook for about 4-5 minutes.
4) With a slotted spoon, transfer the beef cubes into a bowl.
5) In the pot, add the onion and cook for about 3-4 minutes.
6) Add the garlic, ginger, thyme, and curry powder and cook for about 1 minute.
7) Press "Cancel" and stir in the cooked beef and remaining ingredients except for spinach.
8) Cover the pot with "Air Fryer Lid" and seal it.
9) Press "Slow Cook" and set the time for 7 hours.
10) Press "Start" to begin cooking.
11) When cooking time is completed, open the lid, and stir in the spinach.
12) Again, cover the pot with "Air Fryer Lid" and seal it.
13) Press "Slow Cook" and set the time for 30 minutes.
14) Press "Start" to begin cooking.
15) When cooking time is completed, open the lid, and serve hot.

Beef Stuffed Bell Peppers

Prep time: 15 minutes | Cook time: 25 minutes | Serves: 6 | Program: Air Fry | Per Serving: Calories 277

Ingredients:

- Green bell peppers – 6
- Lean ground beef – 1¼ lb.
- Marinara sauce – 1 C.
- Scallion – 1/3 C. chopped
- Fresh parsley – ¼ C. chopped
- Dried sage – ½ tsp. crushed
- Garlic salt – ½ tsp.
- Olive oil – 1 tbsp.
- Mozzarella cheese – ¼ C. shredded

Directions:

1) Cut the top of each bell pepper and carefully, remove the seeds. Set aside.
2) Heat a nonstick skillet over medium-high heat and cook the beef for about 8-10 minutes.
3) Drain the grease completely.
4) Add the marinara sauce, scallion, parsley, sage, salt, and oil and mix well.
5) Stuff each bell pepper with beef mixture.

6) Arrange the greased Air Fryer Basket in the pot of Instant Pot Duo Crisp.
7) Cover the pot with "Air Fryer Lid" and seal it.
8) Press "Air Fry" and set the temperature to 355 °F for 15 minutes.
9) Press "Start" to begin preheating.
10) When the unit shows "Hot" instead of "On", open the lid and place the bell peppers into the basket.
11) Again, seal the lid and press "Start" to begin cooking.
12) After 10 minutes of cooking, top each bell pepper with cheese.
13) When cooking time is completed, open the lid, and serve hot.

Seasoned Pork Tenderloin

Prep time: 10 minutes | Cook time: 29 minutes | Serves: 3 | Program: Bake | Per Serving: Calories 272

Ingredients:

- Pork tenderloin – 1 (12-oz.)
- Mrs. Dash seasoning – 2 tbsp.
- Salt and ground black pepper, as required
- Olive oil – 2 tbsp.
- Beef broth – 2 C.

Directions:

1) Season the pork tenderloin with the Mrs. Dash seasoning, salt, and black pepper evenly.
2) In the pot of Instant Pot Duo Crisp, place the oil and press "Sauté".
3) Press "Start" to begin cooking and heat for about 2-3 minutes.
4) Now add the pork and sear for about 2 minutes per side.
5) Press "Cancel" and transfer the pork tenderloin onto a plate.
6) In the pot of Instant Pot Duo Crisp, pour the broth.
7) Arrange the Multi-Functional Rack in the pot.
8) Cover the pot with "Air Fryer Lid" and seal it.
9) Press "Bake" and set the temperature to 350 °F for 25 minutes.
10) Press "Start" to begin preheating.
11) When the unit shows "Hot" instead of "On", open the lid and place the pork tenderloin over the rack.
12) Again, seal the lid and press "Start" to begin cooking.
13) When cooking time is completed, open the lid, and place the pork tenderloin onto a cutting board.
14) Cut into desired sized slices and serve.

Bacon-Wrapped Tenderloin

Prep time: 10 minutes | Cook time: 30 minutes | Serves: 4 | Program: Air Fry | Per Serving: Calories 504

Ingredients:

- Pork tenderloin – 1 (1½ lb.), trimmed
- Bacon strips – 4
- Dijon mustard – 2 tbsp.

Directions:

1) Coat the tenderloin evenly with mustard.
2) Wrap the pork tenderloin with bacon strips.
3) Arrange the greased Air Fryer Basket in the bottom of Instant Pot Duo Crisp.
4) Cover the pot with "Air Fryer Lid" and seal it.
5) Press "Air Fry" and set the temperature to 360 °F for 30 minutes.
6) Press "Start" to begin preheating.
7) When the unit shows "Hot" instead of "On", open the lid and place the pork tenderloin into the basket.
8) Again, seal the lid and press "Start" to begin cooking.
9) When cooking time is completed, open the lid, and place the pork tenderloin onto a platter for about 5 minutes before slicing.
10) Cut the tenderloin into desired sized slices and serve.

Spicy BBQ Pork Ribs

Prep time: 15 minutes │ Cook time: 28 minutes │ Serves: 8 │ Program: Pressure/ Broil │ Per Serving: Calories 481

Ingredients:

- Brown sugar – 2 tbsp.
- Dry mustard – 1 tbsp.
- Ground cumin – 1 tbsp.
- Red chili powder – 1 tbsp.
- Paprika – 1 tbsp.
- Onion powder – 1 tbsp.
- Garlic powder – 1 tbsp.
- Pork back ribs – 4 lb. trimmed
- Beef broth – 1 C.
- BBQ sauce – 1 C.

Directions:

1) For spice rub: in a bowl, add brown sugar, mustard, celery seeds and spices and mix well.
2) Rub the ribs with spice mixture generously and then, cut ribs into desired sized pieces.
3) In the pot of Instant Pot Duo Crisp, pour 1 C. of water.
4) Arrange the Multi-Functional Rack in the pot.
5) Place the ribs over the rack.
6) Cover the pot with "Pressure Lid" and seal it.
7) Press "Pressure" and set the time for 25 minutes.
8) Press "Start" to begin cooking.
9) When cooking time is completed, do a "Natural" release.
10) Open the lid and transfer the ribs into a bowl.
11) Coat the ribs with BBQ sauce generously.
12) Remove the rack from pot and discard the water.
13) Now, arrange the Broiling Tray in the pot.
14) Place the ribs onto the tray.
15) Now, cover the pot with "Air Fryer Lid" and seal it.
16) Press "Broil" and set the time for 3 minutes.
17) Press "Start" to begin cooking.
18) When cooking time is completed, open the lid, and serve hot.

Simple Pork Chops

Prep time: 10 minutes │ Cook time: 18 minutes │ Serves: 2 │ Program: Broil │ Per Serving: Calories 544

Ingredients:

- Pork chops – 2 (6-oz.) (½-inch thick)
- Dried basil – ¼ tsp. crushed
- Salt and ground black pepper, as required

Directions:

1) Season the pork chops with basil, salt, and black pepper evenly.
2) Arrange the greased Broiling Tray in the bottom of Instant Pot Duo Crisp.
3) Cover the pot with "Air Fryer Lid" and seal it.
4) Press "Broil" and set the time for 18 minutes.
5) Press "Start" to begin preheating.
6) When the unit shows "Hot" instead of "On", open the lid and place the chops onto the tray.
7) Again, seal the lid and press "Start" to begin cooking.
8) After 12 minutes of cooking, flip the chops once.
9) When cooking time is completed, open the lid, and serve hot.

Cheesy Sausage Pasta

Prep time: 15 minutes | Cook time: 23 minutes | Serves: 8 | Program:
Pressure/ Air Fry | Per Serving: Calories 558

Ingredients:

- Olive oil – 1 tsp.
- Italian sausage – ¾ lb.
- Medium onion – 1, chopped
- Garlic – 2 tbsp. minced
- Dried oregano – ½ tsp.
- Dried basil – ½ tsp.
- Red pepper flakes – ½ tsp. crushed
- Salt and ground black pepper, as required
- Pepperoni – 6 oz. sliced
- Canned tomato sauce with basil & garlic – 20 oz.
- Chicken broth – 2 C.
- Red wine – 1 C.
- Uncooked pasta – 16 oz.
- Mozzarella cheese – 8 oz. shredded

Directions:

1) In the pot of Instant Pot Duo Crisp, place the oil and press "Sauté".
2) Press "Start" to begin cooking and heat for about 2-3 minutes.

3) Now add the sausage, onion and garlic and cook for about 6-8 minutes.
4) Add the dried herbs, red pepper flakes, salt and black pepper and cook for about 1 minute.
5) Press "Cancel" and stir in the pepperoni, tomato sauce, broth, and wine.
6) Place the pasta on top and gently press down in the mixture.
7) Cover the pot with "Pressure Lid" and seal it.
8) Press "Pressure" and set the time for 6 minutes.
9) Press "Start" to begin cooking.
10) When cooking time is completed, do a "Quick" release.
11) Open the lid and stir in 1/3 of the cheese.
12) Sprinkle the remaining cheese on top evenly.
13) Now, cover the pot with "Air Fryer Lid" and seal it.
14) Press "Air Fry" and set the temperature to 400 °F for 5 minutes.
15) Press "Start" to begin cooking.
16) When cooking time is completed, open the lid, and serve hot.

Sausage & Beans Soup

Prep time: 15 minutes | Cook time: 6 hours | Serves: 8 | Program: Slow Cook | Per Serving: Calories 429

Ingredients:

- Smoked turkey sausage – 1 lb.
- Mixed dry beans – 1 lb. rinsed, soaked overnight and drained
- Onion – 1, chopped
- Garlic clove – 1, minced
- Diced tomatoes with liquid – 1 (28-oz.) can
- Chicken broth – 4 C.
- Water – 2 C.
- Ground black pepper, as required

Directions:

1) In the pot of Instant Pot Duo Crisp, add all ingredients and stir to combine.
2) Cover the pot with "Air Fryer Lid" and seal it.
3) Press "Slow Cook" and set the time for 6 hours.
4) Press "Start" to begin cooking.
5) When cooking time is completed, open the lid, and serve hot.

Herbed Leg of Lamb

Prep time: 15 minutes │ Cook time: 1¼ hours │ Serves: 6 │ Program: Air Fry │ Per Serving: Calories 358

Ingredients:

- Boneless leg of lamb – 2¼ lb.

- Olive oil – 2 tbsp.
- Salt and ground black pepper, as required
- Fresh rosemary sprigs – 4

Directions:

1) Coat the leg of lamb with oil and sprinkle with salt and black pepper.
2) Wrap the leg of lamb with herb sprigs.
3) Arrange the Multi-Functional Rack in the pot of Instant Pot Duo Crisp.
4) Cover the pot with "Air Fryer Lid" and seal it.
5) Press "Air Fry" and set the temperature to 300 °F for 75 minutes.
6) Press "Start" to begin preheating.
7) When the unit shows "Hot" instead of "On", open the lid and place the leg of lamb over the rack.
8) Again, seal the lid and press "Start" to begin cooking.
9) When cooking time is completed, open the lid, and place the leg of lamb onto a cutting board.
10) Cut into desired sized pieces and serve.

Garlicky Lamb Shanks

Prep time: 10 minutes | Cook time: 45 minutes | Serves: 2 | Program: Pressure | Per Serving: Calories 980

Ingredients:

- Lamb shanks – 2 lb. trimmed
- Salt and ground black pepper, as required
- Olive oil – 1 tbsp.
- Whole garlic cloves – 4, peeled
- Chicken broth – 1 C.
- Tomato paste – 1 tbsp.
- Dried rosemary – ½ tsp. crushed
- Fresh lemon juice – 2 tbsp.
- Unsalted butter – 1 tbsp.

Directions:

1) Season the shanks with salt and pepper.
2) In the pot of Instant Pot Duo Crisp, place the oil and press "Sauté".
3) Press "Start" to begin cooking and heat for about 2-3 minutes.
4) Now add the shanks and sear for about 2-3 minutes per side or until browned completely.
5) Add the garlic cloves and cook for about 1 minute.
6) Press "Cancel" to stop cooking and stir in the remaining ingredients.
7) Cover the pot with "Pressure Lid" and seal it.
8) Press "Pressure" and set the time for 30 minutes.
9) Press "Start" to begin cooking.
10) When cooking time is completed, do a "Natural" release.
11) Open the lid and with tongs, transfer the lamb shanks onto a platter.
12) Press "Sauté" of pot and then press "Start" to begin cooking.
13) Cook for about 5 minutes.
14) Add in the lemon juice and butter and stir until smooth.
15) Press "Cancel" to stop cooking and pour sauce over shanks.

16) Serve immediately.

Almond Crusted Rack of Lamb

Prep time: 15 minutes | Cook time: 35 minutes | Serves: 6 | Program: Air Fry | Per Serving: Calories 319

Ingredients:

- Rack of lamb – 1¾ lb.
- Salt and ground black pepper, as required
- Egg – 1
- Breadcrumbs – 1 tbsp.
- Almonds – 3 oz. chopped finely

Directions:

1) Season the rack of lamb with salt and black pepper evenly and then, drizzle with cooking spray.
2) In a shallow dish, beat the egg.
3) In another shallow dish mix together breadcrumbs and almonds.
4) Dip the rack of lamb in egg and then coat with the almond mixture.
5) Arrange the greased Air Fryer Basket in the pot of Instant Pot Duo Crisp.
6) Cover the pot with "Air Fryer Lid" and seal it.
7) Press "Air Fry" and set the temperature to 220 °F for 30 minutes.

8) Press "Start" to begin preheating.
9) When the unit shows "Hot" instead of "On", open the lid and place the lamb rack into the basket.
10) Again, seal the lid and press "Start" to begin cooking.
11) After 30 minutes of cooking, set the temperature to 390 °F for 5 minutes.
12) When cooking time is completed, open the lid, and serve hot.

Glazed Lamb Chops

Prep time: 10 minutes | Cook time: 15 minutes | Serves: 4 | Program: Bake | Per Serving: Calories 224

Ingredients:

- Dijon mustard – 1 tbsp.
- Fresh lime juice – ½ tbsp.
- Honey – 1 tsp.
- Olive oil – ½ tsp.
- Salt and ground black pepper, as required
- Lamb loin chops – 4 (4-oz.)

Directions:

1) In a large bowl, mix together the mustard, lime juice, oil, honey, salt, and black pepper.
2) Add the chops and coat with the mixture generously.
3) Place the chops into a greased baking dish.

4) Arrange the Multi-Functional Rack in the pot of Instant Pot Duo Crisp.
5) Cover the pot with "Air Fryer Lid" and seal it.
6) Press "Bake" and set the temperature to 390 °F for 15 minutes.
7) Press "Start" to begin preheating.
8) When the unit shows "Hot" instead of "On", open the lid and place the baking dish over the rack.
9) Again, seal the lid and press "Start" to begin cooking.
10) While cooking, flip the chops once halfway through.
11) When cooking time is completed, open the lid, and serve hot.

Cheesy Lamb Burgers

Prep time: 15 minutes | Cook time: 5 minutes | Serves: 2 | Program: Pressure | Per Serving: Calories 544

Ingredients:

- Lean ground lamb – 1 lb.
- Worcestershire sauce – 1 tbsp.
- Salt and ground black pepper, as required
- Cheddar cheese – 2 oz. shredded

Directions:

1) In a large bowl, add the ground lamb, Worcestershire Sauce, salt, and black pepper and mix until well combined.
2) Make 4 equal-sized balls from the mixture and with your hands, flatten each ball.
3) Place 1 oz. of the cheese in the center of 2 of the flattened balls.
4) Cover each with the remaining 2 flattened balls, pressing the edges together well.
5) In the pot of Instant Pot Duo Crisp, place ½ C. of water.
6) Arrange the Multi-Functional Rack in the pot.
7) Place the patties over the rack.
8) Cover the pot with "Pressure Lid" and seal it.
9) Press "Pressure" and set the time for 5 minutes.
10) Press "Start" to begin cooking.
11) When cooking time is completed, do a "Natural" release.
12) Open the lid and serve hot.

Lamb Meatloaf

Prep time: 15 minutes | Cook time: 6 hours | Serves: 6 | Program: Slow Cook | Per Serving: Calories 262

Ingredients:

- Medium onion – 1, minced
- Garlic cloves – 3, minced
- Lean ground lamb – 1½ lb.

- Almond flour – ¾ C.
- Mozzarella cheese – 1 C. shredded
- Large eggs – 2
- Worcestershire sauce – 2 tsp.
- Salt and ground black pepper, as required
- Olive oil cooking spray
- Tomato sauce – ¼ C.

Directions:

1) In a bowl, add all the ingredients except for the tomato sauce and mix until well combined.
2) Lightly grease pot of Instant Pot Duo Crisp with cooking liquid.
3) In the prepared pot, place the lamb mixture and shape into an oval.
4) Cover the meatloaf with tomato sauce.
5) Cover the pot with "Air Fryer Lid" and seal it.
6) Press "Slow Cook" and set the time for 6 hours.
7) Press "Start" to begin cooking.
8) When cooking time is completed, open the lid, and place the meatloaf onto a cutting board.
9) Cut into desired sized slices and serve.

Fish & Seafood Recipes

Simple Salmon

Prep time: 10 minutes | Cook time: 5 minutes | Serves: 2 | Program: Steam | Per Serving: Calories 191

Ingredients:

- Salmon fillets – 2 (5-oz.)
- Salt and ground black pepper, as required
- Fresh lemon juice – 2 tbsp.

Directions:

1) Season the salmon fillets with salt and black pepper evenly.
2) In the pot of Instant Pot Duo Crisp, place 1 C. of water.
3) Arrange the Multi-Functional Rack in the pot.
4) Place the salmon fillets over the rack.
5) Cover the pot with "Pressure Lid" and seal it.
6) Press "Steam" and set the time for 5 minutes.
7) Press "Start" to begin cooking.
8) When cooking time is completed, do a "Quick" release.
9) Open the lid and transfer the salmon onto serving plates.
10) Drizzle with lemon juice and serve.

Honey Glazed Salmon

Prep time: 10 minutes | Cook time: 13 minutes | Serves: 2 | Program: Air Fry | Per Serving: Calories 220

Ingredients:

- Soy sauce – 1 tbsp.
- Chili garlic sauce – 1 tbsp.
- Honey – 2 tbsp.
- Fresh lemon juice – 2 tsp.
- Water – 2 tsp.
- Salmon fillets – 2 (4-oz.)

Directions:

1) In a small bowl, place all the ingredients except the salmon and mix well.
2) In a small bowl, reserve about half of the mixture.
3) Add the salmon in remaining mixture and coat well.
4) Refrigerate, covered to marinate for about 2 hours.
5) Arrange the greased Air Fryer Basket in the pot of Instant Pot Duo Crisp.
6) Cover the pot with "Air Fryer Lid" and seal it.
7) Press "Air Fry" and set the temperature to 355 °F for 13 minutes.
8) Press "Start" to begin preheating.

9) When the unit shows "Hot" instead of "On", open the lid and place the salmon fillets into the basket.
10) Again, seal the lid and press "Start" to begin cooking.
11) After 8 minutes, flip the salmon fillets and coat with reserved marinade.
12) When cooking time is completed, open the lid, and serve hot.

Pesto Salmon

Prep time: 10 minutes | Cook time: 20 minutes | Serves: 4 | Program: Air Fry | Per Serving: Calories 380

Ingredients:

- Salmon fillets – 4 (6-oz.)
- Olive oil – 2 tsp.
- Pinch of salt
- Pesto – ½ C.

Directions:

1) Drizzle the salmon fillets with oil evenly and sprinkle with a pinch of salt.
2) Arrange the greased Air Fryer Basket in the bottom of Instant Pot Duo Crisp.
3) Cover the pot with "Air Fryer Lid" and seal it.
4) Press "Air Fry" and set the temperature to 270 °F for 20 minutes.

5) Press "Start" to begin preheating.
6) When the unit shows "Hot" instead of "On", open the lid and place the salmon fillets into the basket.
7) Again, seal the lid and press "Start" to begin cooking.
8) When cooking time is completed, open the lid, and place the salmon fillets onto a platter.
9) Top with the pesto and serve immediately.

Salmon in Dill Sauce

Prep time: 10 minutes | Cook time: 2 hours | Serves: 6 | Program: Slow Cook | Per Serving: Calories 164

Ingredients:

- Water – 2 C.
- Chicken broth – 1 C.
- Fresh lemon juice – 2 tbsp.
- Fresh dill – ¼ C. chopped
- Lemon zest – ½ tsp. grated
- Salmon fillets – 6 (4-oz.)
- Cayenne pepper – 1 tsp.
- Salt and ground black pepper, as required

Directions:

1) In the pot of Instant Pot Duo Crisp, mix together the water, broth, lemon juice, dill and lemon zest.

2) Arrange the salmon fillets on top, skin side down and sprinkle with cayenne pepper, salt, and black pepper.
3) Cover the pot with "Air Fryer Lid" and seal it.
4) Press "Slow Cook" and set the time for 2 hours.
5) Press "Start" to begin cooking.
6) When cooking time is completed, open the lid, and serve hot.

Parmesan Tilapia

Prep time: 15 minutes ｜ Cook time: 4 hours ｜ Serves: 4 ｜ Program: Slow Cook ｜ Per Serving: Calories 190

Ingredients:

- Parmesan cheese – ½ C. grated
- Mayonnaise – ¼ C.
- Fresh lemon juice – ¼ C.
- Salt and ground black pepper, as required
- Tilapia fillets – 4 (4-oz.)
- Fresh cilantro – 2 tbsp. chopped

Directions:

1) In a bowl, mix together all ingredients except tilapia fillets and cilantro.
1) Coat the fillets with mayonnaise mixture evenly.
2) Place the filets on a large piece of foil.
3) Wrap the foil around fillets to seal them.

4) Arrange the foil packet in the pot of Instant Pot Duo Crisp.
5) Cover the pot with "Air Fryer Lid" and seal it.
6) Press "Slow Cook" and set the time for 4 hours.
7) Press "Start" to begin cooking.
8) When cooking time is completed, open the lid, and transfer the foil packet onto a platter.
9) Carefully open the parcel and serve hot with the garnishing of cilantro.

Cod with Tomatoes

Prep time: 10 minutes | Cook time: 6 minutes | Serves: 4 | Program: Pressure | Per Serving: Calories 149

Ingredients:

- Cherry tomatoes – 1 lb. halved
- Fresh rosemary – 2 tbsp. chopped
- Cod fillets – 4 (4-oz.)
- Garlic cloves – 2, minced
- Olive oil – 1 tbsp.
- Salt and ground black pepper, as required

Directions:

1) In the bottom of a greased a large heatproof bowl, place half of the cherry tomatoes followed by the rosemary.

2) Arrange cod fillets on top in a single layer, followed by the remaining tomatoes.
3) Sprinkle with garlic and drizzle with oil.
4) In the pot of Instant Pot Duo Crisp, arrange the bowl.
5) Cover the pot with "Pressure Lid" and seal it.
6) Press "Pressure" and set the time for 6 minutes.
7) Press "Start" to begin cooking.
8) When cooking time is completed, do a "Quick" release.
9) Open the lid and transfer the fish fillets and tomatoes onto serving plates.
10) Sprinkle with salt and black pepper and serve.

Spicy Trout

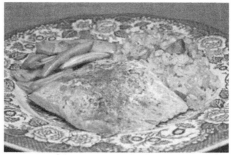

Prep time: 10 minutes | Cook time: 5 minutes | Serves: 2 | Program: Steam | Per Serving: Calories 271

Ingredients:

- Garam masala powder – ¼ tsp.
- Ground cumin – ¼ tsp.
- Ground coriander – ¼ tsp.
- Ground turmeric – ¼ tsp.
- Salt and ground black pepper, as required
- Trout fillets – 2 (5-oz.)

Directions:

1) In a bowl, mix together the spices.

2) Rub the trout fillets with spice mixture generously.
3) In the pot of Instant Pot Duo Crisp, place 1 C. of water.
4) Arrange the Multi-Functional Rack in the pot.
5) Place the trout fillets over the rack.
6) Cover the pot with "Pressure Lid" and seal it.
7) Press "Steam" and set the time for 5 minutes.
8) Press "Start" to begin cooking.
9) When cooking time is completed, do a "Quick" release.
10) Open the lid and serve immediately.

Fish Curry

Prep time: 15 minutes | Cook time: 15 minutes | Serves: 5 | Program: Pressure | Per Serving: Calories 323

Ingredients:

- Olive oil – 1 tbsp.
- Curry leaves – 2
- Medium onions – 2, chopped
- Fresh ginger – 1 tbsp. grated finely
- Garlic cloves – 2, minced
- Curry powder – 2 tbsp.
- Ground cumin – 2 tsp.
- Ground coriander – 2 tsp.
- Red chili powder – 1 tsp.
- Ground turmeric – ½ tsp.

- Unsweetened coconut milk – 2 C.
- White fish fillets – 1½ lb. cut into bite-sized pieces
- Tomatoes – 1¼ C. chopped
- Serrano pepper – 1, seeded and chopped
- Fresh lemon juice – 1 tbsp.

Directions:

1) In the pot of Instant Pot Duo Crisp, place the oil and press "Sauté".
2) Press "Start" to begin cooking and heat for about 2-3 minutes.
3) Now add the curry leaves and cook for about 30 seconds.
4) Add onion, ginger and garlic and cook for about 4-5 minutes.
5) Add spices and cook for about 1½ minutes.
6) Add the coconut milk and stir to combine.
7) Press "Cancel" and stir in fish, tomatoes, and Serrano pepper.
8) Cover the pot with "Pressure Lid" and seal it.
9) Press "Pressure" and set the time for 5 minutes.
10) Press "Start" to begin cooking.
11) When cooking time is completed, do a "Natural" release.
12) Remove the lid and stir in the lemon juice.
13) Serve hot.

Shrimp Scampi

Prep time: 15 minutes | Cook time: 7 minutes | Serves: 3 | Program: Air Fry | Per Serving: Calories 245

Ingredients:

- Salted butter – 4 tbsp.
- Fresh lemon juice – 1 tbsp.
- Garlic – 1 tbsp. minced
- Red pepper flakes – 2 tsp. crushed
- Shrimp – 1 lb. peeled and deveined
- Fresh basil – 2 tbsp. chopped
- Fresh chives – 1 tbsp. chopped
- Chicken broth – 2 tbsp.

Directions:

1) Arrange a 7-inch round baking pan in the Air Fryer Basket.
2) Arrange the greased Air Fryer Basket in the bottom of Instant Pot Duo Crisp.
3) Cover the pot with "Air Fryer Lid" and seal it.
4) Press "Air Fry" and set the temperature to 325 °F for 7 minutes.
5) Press "Start" to begin preheating.
6) When the unit shows "Hot" instead of "On", open the lid and carefully remove the pan from pot.

7) In the heated pan, place butter, lemon juice, garlic, and red pepper flakes and mix well.
8) Again, place the pan into the basket.
9) Again, seal the lid and press "Start" to begin cooking.
10) After 2 minutes of cooking in the baking pan, stir in the shrimp, basil, chives, and broth.
11) When cooking time is completed, open the lid, and place the pan onto a wire rack for about 1 minute.
12) Stir the mixture and serve hot.

Vanilla Shrimp

Prep time: 15 minutes | Cook time: 30 minutes | Serves: 3 | Program: Sous Vide | Per Serving: Calories 105

Ingredients:

- Vanilla bean – 1
- large shrimp – 12, peeled and deveined
- Paprika – ¼ tsp.
- Salt and ground black pepper, as required

Directions:

1) Fill the pot of Instant Pot Duo Crisp with water up to ½-full mark .
2) Press "Sous Vide" and set the temperature to 136 °F for 30 minutes.

3) Cover the pot with "Pressure Lid" and press "Start " to preheat.
4) Meanwhile, split the vanilla bean in half and scrape out the seeds.
5) In a bowl, add shrimp, vanilla seeds, paprika, salt and pepper and toss to coat.
6) In a cooking pouch, place the shrimp mixture.
7) Seal the pouch tightly after squeezing out the excess air.
8) When the unit shows "Hot" instead of "On", open the lid and place the pouch in the pot.
9) Again, seal the lid and press "Start" to begin cooking.
10) When the cooking time is completed, open the lid, and remove the pouch from inner pot.
11) Carefully open the pouch and transfer the shrimp with cooking liquid into a serving bowl.
12) Serve hot.

Shrimp with Tomatoes

Prep time: 15 minutes | Cook time: 5¼ minutes | Serves: 4 | Program: Slow Cook | Per Serving: Calories 315

Ingredients:

- Peeled tomatoes – 1 (14-oz.) can, chopped finely
- Canned tomato paste – 4 oz.
- Garlic cloves – 2, minced
- Fresh parsley – 2 tbsp. chopped

- Salt and ground black pepper, as required
- Lemon pepper – 1 tsp.
- Cooked shrimp – 2 lb. peeled and deveined

Directions:

1) In the pot of Instant Pot Duo Crisp, add all the ingredients except for shrimp and stir to combine.
2) Cover the pot with "Air Fryer Lid" and seal it.
3) Press "Slow Cook" and set the time for 5 hours.
4) Press "Start" to begin cooking.
5) When cooking time is completed, open the lid, and stir in the shrimp.
6) Again, cover the pot with "Air Fryer Lid" and seal it.
7) Press "Slow Cook" and set the time for 15 minutes.
8) Press "Start" to begin cooking.
9) When cooking time is completed, open the lid, and serve hot.

Herbed Scallops

Prep time: 10 minutes | Cook time: 4 minutes | Serves: 2 | Program: Air Fry | Per Serving: Calories 203

Ingredients:

- Sea scallops – ¾ lb. cleaned and pat dry
- Butter – 1 tbsp. melted
- Fresh rosemary – ¼ tbsp. chopped

- Fresh thyme – ¼ tbsp. chopped
- Salt and ground black pepper, as required

Directions:

1) In a large bowl, place the scallops, butter, herbs, salt, and black pepper and toss to coat well.
2) Arrange the greased Air Fryer Basket in the pot of Instant Pot Duo Crisp.
3) Cover the pot with "Air Fryer Lid" and seal it.
4) Press "Air Fry" and set the temperature to 390 °F for 4 minutes.
5) Press "Start" to begin preheating.
6) When the unit shows "Hot" instead of "On", open the lid and place the scallops into the basket.
7) Again, seal the lid and press "Start" to begin cooking.
8) When cooking time is completed, open the lid, and serve hot.

Lemony Mussels

Prep time: 15 minutes | Cook time: 10 minutes | Serves: 4 | Program: Pressure | Per Serving: Calories 249

Ingredients:

- Olive oil – 1 tbsp.
- Medium yellow onion – 1, chopped
- Garlic clove – 1, minced

123

- Dried rosemary – ½ tsp. crushed
- Chicken broth – 1 C.
- Fresh lemon juice – 2 tbsp.
- Salt and ground black pepper, as required
- Mussels – 2 lb. cleaned and de-bearded

Directions:

1) In the pot of Instant Pot Duo Crisp, place the oil and press "Sauté".
2) Press "Start" to begin cooking and heat for about 2-3 minutes.
3) Now add the onion and cook for about 5 minutes.
4) Add the garlic and rosemary and cook for about 1 minute.
5) Press "Cancel" and stir in the broth, lemon juice and black pepper.
6) Arrange the Multi-Functional Rack over the broth mixture.
7) Place the mussels over the rack.
8) Cover the pot with "Pressure Lid" and seal it.
9) Press "Pressure" and set the time for 1 minute.
10) Press "Start" to begin cooking.
11) When cooking time is completed, do a "Quick" release.
12) Remove the lid and transfer the mussels into a serving bowl.
13) Top with the cooking liquid and serve.

Creamy Lobster Tails

Prep time: 15 minutes | Cook time: 3 minutes | Serves: 3 | Program: Pressure | Per Serving: Calories 582

Ingredients:

- Old bay seasoning – 1 tsp.
- Fresh lobster tails – 2 lb.
- Scallion – 1, chopped
- Mayonnaise – ½ C.
- Unsalted butter – 2 tbsp. melted
- Fresh lemon juice – 2 tbsp. divided

Directions:

1) In the pot of Instant Pot Duo Crisp, place 1½ C. of water and 1-2 pinches of old bay seasoning.
2) Arrange the Multi-Functional Rack in the pot.
3) Arrange the lobster tail over the rack, shell side down, meat side up.
4) Drizzle the lobster tails with 1 tbsp. of lemon juice.
5) Cover the pot with "Pressure Lid" and seal it.
6) Press "Pressure" and set the time for 3 minutes.
7) Press "Start" to begin cooking.
8) When cooking time is completed, do a "Quick" release.
9) Open the lid and transfer the tails into the bowl of ice bath for about 1 minute.

10) With kitchen shears, cut the underbelly of the tail down the center.
11) Remove the meat and chop it up into large chunks.
12) In a large bowl, add the lobster meat, scallions, mayonnaise, butter, seasoning and lemon juice and mix well.
13) Refrigerate for at least 15 minutes before serving.

Herbed Seafood Stew

Prep time: 20 minutes | Cook time: 4¾ hours | Serves: 8 | Program: Slow Cook | Per Serving: Calories 228

Ingredients:

- Celery stalk – 1, chopped
- Yellow onion – 1, chopped
- Garlic cloves – 3, chopped
- Fresh cilantro leaves – 1 C. chopped
- Tomatoes – 1 C. chopped finely
- Chicken broth – 4 C.
- Fresh lemon juice – 2 tbsp.
- Olive oil – 2 tbsp.
- Mixed dried herbs – 3 tsp.
- Salt and ground black pepper, as required
- Cod fillets – 1 lb. cubed
- Shrimp – 1 lb. peeled and deveined

- Scallops – 1 lb.
- Crabmeat – ¾ C.

Directions:

1) In the pot of Instant Pot Duo Crisp, add all ingredients except for seafood and mix well.
2) Cover the pot with "Air Fryer Lid" and seal it.
3) Press "Slow Cook" and set the time for 4 hours.
4) Press "Start" to begin cooking.
5) When cooking time is completed, open the lid, and stir in the seafood.
6) Again, cover the pot with "Air Fryer Lid" and seal it.
7) Press "Slow Cook" and set the time for 45 minutes.
8) Press "Start" to begin cooking.
9) When cooking time is completed, open the lid, and serve hot.

Dessert Recipes

Wine Poached Pears

Prep time: 15 minutes | Cook time: 2 hours | Serves: 4 | Program: Sous Vide | Per Serving: Calories 276

Ingredients:

- Ripe pears – 4, peeled
- Red wine – 1 C.
- Sweet vermouth – ¼ C.
- Granulated sugar – ½ C.
- Salt – 1 tsp.
- Orange zest – 1 (3-inch) piece
- Vanilla bean – 1, seeds scraped

Directions:

1) Fill the pot of Instant Pot Duo Crisp with water up to ½-full mark .
2) Press "Sous Vide" and set the temperature to 175 °F for 1 hour.
3) Cover the pot with "Pressure Lid" and press "Start " to preheat.
4) In a cooking pouch, place all ingredients. Seal the pouch tightly after squeezing out the excess air.

5) When the unit shows "Hot" instead of "On", open the lid and place the pouch in the pot.
6) Again, seal the lid and press "Start" to begin cooking.
7) When the cooking time is completed, open the lid, and remove the pouch from inner pot.
8) Carefully open the pouch and transfer the pears onto serving plates.
9) Drizzle with some of the cooking liquid and serve.

Chocolate Pots de Crème

Prep time: 10 minutes | Cook time: 9 minutes | Serves: 6 | Program: Pressure | Per Serving: Calories 392

Ingredients:

- Heavy cream – 1½ C.
- Milk – ½ C.
- Sugar – ¼ C.
- Large egg yolks – 5
- Pinch of salt
- Dark chocolate – 8 oz. melted

Directions:

1) In a small pan, add the cream and milk and bring to a gentle simmer.
2) Immediately, remove from the heat.

3) In a bowl, add sugar, egg yolks and salt and beat until well combined.
4) Slowly add the warmed cream mixture into egg yolk mixture, beating continuously.
5) Add the melted chocolate and stir to combine.
6) Divide the mixture into 6 custard cups evenly.
7) With a foil piece, cover each custard cup.
8) In the pot of Instant Pot Duo Crisp, place 1 C. of water.
9) Arrange a Multi-Functional Rack in the pot.
10) Place 3 custard cups over the rack.
11) Arrange a second rack on top.
12) Place remaining 3 custard cups on top of second rack.
13) Cover the pot with "Pressure Lid" and seal it.
14) Press "Pressure" and set the time for 6 minutes.
15) Press "Start" to begin cooking.
16) When cooking time is completed, do a "Natural" release.
17) Open the lid and place the custard cups onto a wire rack.
18) Remove the foil pieces and let them cool.
19) With a plastic wrap, cover each ramekin and refrigerate to chill for at least 4 hours before serving.

Vanilla Custard

Prep time: 150 minutes | Cook time: 2 hours | Serves: 6 | Program: Slow Cook | Per Serving: Calories 145

Ingredients:

- Heavy cream – 1 C.
- Unsweetened almond milk – ½ C.
- Sugar – ¼ C.
- Eggs – 2
- Egg yolks – 2
- Vanilla extract – 1 tsp.
- Ground cinnamon – ½ tsp.
- Salt – ¼ tsp.

Directions:

1) In the bowl of a stand mixer, add all the ingredients and beat over medium-high speed until well combined.
2) Place the mixture into greased 6 (4-oz.) ramekins evenly about ¾ of the way full.
3) In the pot of Instant Pot Duo Crisp, arrange the ramekins.
4) Cover the pot with "Air Fryer Lid" and seal it.
5) Press "Slow Cook" and set the time for 2 hours.
6) Press "Start" to begin cooking.
7) When cooking time is completed, open the lid, and place the ramekins onto a wire rack to cool for about 1 hour.
8) Refrigerate for about 2 hours before serving.

Rice Pudding

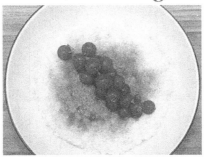

Prep time: 10 minutes | Cook time: 20 minutes | Serves: 6 | Program: Pressure | Per Serving: Calories 291

Ingredients:

- Whole milk – 5 C.
- Medium-grain white rice – ½ C.
- Sugar – ½ C.
- Mixed nuts (cashews, almonds, walnut, pistachios) – 1/3 C. chopped
- Ground cardamom – 1 tsp.

Directions:

1) In the pot of Instant Pot Duo Crisp, mix together all ingredients.
2) Cover the pot with "Pressure Lid" and seal it.
3) Press "Pressure" and set the time for 20 minutes.
4) Press "Start" to begin cooking.
5) When cooking time is completed, do a "Natural" release.
6) Open the lid and transfer the pudding in to serving bowls.
7) Set aside to cool for about 10 minutes.
8) Serve warm.

Apple Pastries

Prep time: 15 minutes | Cook time: 10 minutes | Serves: 8 | Program: Air Fry | Per Serving: Calories 148

Ingredients:

- Large apple – ½, peeled, cored, and chopped
- Fresh orange zest – 1 tsp. grated finely
- White sugar – ½ tbsp.
- Ground cinnamon – ½ tsp.
- Prepared frozen puff pastry – 7.05 oz.

Directions:

1) Place all ingredients except for puff pastry in a bowl and mix well.
2) Cut the pastry in 16 squares.
3) Place about 1 tsp. of the apple mixture in the center of each square.
4) Fold each square into a triangle and press the edges slightly with wet fingers.
5) Then with a fork, press the edges firmly.
6) Arrange the greased Air Fryer Basket in the pot of Instant Pot Duo Crisp.
7) Cover the pot with "Air Fryer Lid" and seal it.
8) Press "Air Fry" and set the temperature to 390 °F for 10 minutes.
9) Press "Start" to begin preheating.
10) When the unit shows "Hot" instead of "On", open the lid and place the pastries into the basket.
11) Again, seal the lid and press "Start" to begin cooking.
12) When cooking time is completed, open the lid, and serve warm.

Blueberry Muffins

Prep time: 15 minutes | Cook time: 25 minutes | Serves: 6 | Program: Bake | Per Serving: Calories 96

Ingredients:

- Whole-wheat flour – 1/3 C.
- Cornmeal – 1/3 C.
- Baking powder – 2 tsp.
- Ground cinnamon – ½ tsp.
- Salt – ¼ tsp.
- Large egg – 1
- Buttermilk – ½ C.
- Unsweetened applesauce – 2 tbsp.
- Sugar – 2 tbsp.
- Fresh blueberries – ½ C.

Directions:

1) Grease 6 cups of a muffin tin and set aside.
2) In a bowl, mix together the flour, cornmeal, baking powder, cinnamon, and salt.
3) In a small bowl, place the egg, buttermilk, applesauce, and sugar and beat until well combined.
4) Add the flour mixture and mix until just combined.
5) Gently, fold in the blueberries.
6) Divide the mixture into prepared muffin cups evenly.

7) Arrange the Multi-Functional Rack in the pot of Instant Pot Duo Crisp.
8) Cover the pot with "Air Fryer Lid" and seal it.
9) Press "Bake" and set the temperature to 350 °F for 25 minutes.
10) Press "Start" to begin preheating.
11) When the unit shows "Hot" instead of "On", open the lid and place the muffin tin over the rack.
12) Again, seal the lid and press "Start" to begin cooking.
13) When cooking time is completed, open the lid, and place the muffin tin onto a wire rack to cool for about 10 minutes.
14) Carefully invert the muffins onto the wire rack to completely cool before serving.

Lava Cake

Prep time: 10 minutes ╷ Cook time: 20 minutes ╷ Serves: 2 ╷ Program: Air Fry ╷ Per Serving: Calories 122

Ingredients:

- Egg – 1
- Unsweetened cocoa powder – 2 tbsp.
- Golden flax meal – 1 tbsp.
- Erythritol – 2 tbsp.
- Stevia powder – 1/8 tsp.
- Water – 2 tbsp.

135

- Coconut oil – 1 tbsp. melted
- Baking powder – ½ tsp.
- Dash of vanilla extract
- Pinch of salt

Directions:

1) In a small glass Pyrex dish, place all the ingredients and beat until well combined.
2) Arrange the greased Air Fryer Basket in the pot of Instant Pot Duo Crisp.
3) Cover the pot with "Air Fryer Lid" and seal it.
4) Press "Air Fry" and set the temperature to 350 °F for 20 minutes.
5) Press "Start" to begin preheating.
6) When the unit shows "Hot" instead of "On", open the lid and place the Pyrex dish into the basket.
7) Again, seal the lid and press "Start" to begin cooking.
8) When cooking time is completed, open the lid, and place the Pyrex dish onto a wire rack to cool for about 10 minutes.
9) Serve warm.

Blueberry Cake

Prep time: 15 minutes | Cook time: 25 minutes | Serves: 8 | Program: Bake | Per Serving: Calories 337

Ingredients:

- All-purpose flour – 2 C.
- Fresh blueberries – 2 C.
- Sugar – ¾ C. plus 3 tbsp.
- Unsalted butter – 8 tbsp. softened
- Egg – 1
- Vanilla extract – 1 tsp.
- Baking powder – 2 tsp.
- Salt – 1 tsp.
- Buttermilk – ½ C.

Directions:

1) In a bowl, add ¼ C. of flour and blueberries and toss to coat well. Set aside.
2) In a second bowl, add the remaining flour, baking powder and salt and mix well.
3) In a third bowl, add the sugar and butter and with an electric mixer, beat until light and fluffy.
4) Add the egg and vanilla extract and beat until well combined.
5) Add half of the flour mixture and gently, stir to combine.
6) Add the remaining flour mixture and gently, stir to combine.
7) Add the buttermilk and mix well.
8) Fold in the blueberries.
9) Place the mixture into a greased cake pan.
10) Arrange the Multi-Functional Rack in the pot of Instant Pot Duo Crisp.
11) Cover the pot with "Air Fryer Lid" and seal it.
12) Press "Bake" and set the temperature to 350 °F for 25 minutes.

13) Press "Start" to begin preheating.
14) When the unit shows "Hot" instead of "On", open the lid and place the baking dish over the rack.
15) Again, seal the lid and press "Start" to begin cooking.
16) When cooking time is completed, open the lid, and place the pan onto a wire rack to cool for about 10 minutes.
17) Carefully invert the cake onto the wire rack to cool completely.
18) Cut into desired sized slices and serve.

Apple Crisp

Prep time: 15 minutes | Cook time: 11 minutes | Serves: 4 | Program: Pressure | Per Serving: Calories 257

Ingredients:

- Old-fashioned rolled oats – ¾ C.
- Butter – 4 tbsp. melted
- All-purpose flour – ¼ C.
- Brown sugar – ¼ C.
- Salt – ¼ tsp.
- Medium apples – 5, peeled, cored, and cut into chunks
- Ground cinnamon – 2 tsp.
- Ground nutmeg – ½ tsp.
- Water – ½ C.
- Honey – 1 tbsp.

Directions:

1) In a bowl, add oats, butter, flour, brown sugar, and salt and mix well.
2) In the pot of Instant Pot Duo Crisp, place apple chunks and sprinkle with cinnamon and nutmeg.
3) Top with water and honey.
4) With a spoonful, drop oats mixture on top of the apples.
5) Cover the pot with "Pressure Lid" and seal it.
6) Press "Pressure" and set the time for 8 minutes.
7) Press "Start" to begin cooking.
8) When cooking time is completed, do a "Natural" release.
9) Open the lid and serve warm.

Fruity Cobbler

Prep time: 15 minutes | Cook time: 15 minutes | Serves: 4 | Program: Steam | Per Serving: Calories 256

Ingredients:

- Plum – 1, pitted and chopped
- Apple 1, cored and chopped
- Pear 1, cored and chopped
- Coconut oil 3 tbsp. melted
- Raw honey 2 tbsp.
- Ground cinnamon ½ tsp.
- Pecans ¼ C. chopped

- Unsweetened coconut ¼ C. shredded
- Sunflower seeds 2 tbsp. roasted

Directions:

1) In a bowl, mix together all fruit.
2) In the pot of Instant Pot Duo Crisp, place the fruit and drizzle with coconut oil and honey.
3) Sprinkle with cinnamon.
4) Cover the pot with "Pressure Lid" and seal it.
5) Press "Steam" and set the time for 10 minutes.
6) Press "Start" to begin cooking.
7) When cooking time is completed, do a "Quick" release.
8) Open the lid and with a slotted spoon, transfer the cooked fruit into a serving bowl.
9) Press "Sauté" of pot and stir in the pecans, coconut, and sunflower seeds.
10) Press "Start" to begin cooking and cook for about 5 minutes, stirring continuously.
11) Press "Cancel" to stop cooking and place the pecan mixture over the cooked fruit.
12) Serve warm.

Conclusion

Instant Pot Duo Crisp 11 in 1 is a genius device to aid you in the kitchen. It takes little space and is very easy to use. Moreover, it comes with 10+ safety features. So, even a first-timer can use it without endangering themself. You can use the Instant Pot Duo Crisp 11 in 1 to cook rice, make a cake or dessert and perform other versatile functions. It has Even Crisp technology that makes your food extra flavorful and crispy to taste. You can now cook in an incredibly fast time and still get awesome results!

Made in United States
Orlando, FL
20 August 2022

21293861R00078